The Singer's Companion

The Singer's Companion

Sharon Stohrer

Routledge
Taylor & Francis Group

New York   London

Published in 2006 by
Routledge
Taylor & Francis Group
270 Madison Avenue
New York, NY 10016

Published in Great Britain by
Routledge
Taylor & Francis Group
2 Park Square
Milton Park, Abingdon
Oxon OX14 4RN

Printed in the United States of America on acid-free paper
10 9 8 7 6 5 4 3 2 1

International Standard Book Number-10: 0-415-97697-9 (Hardcover) 0-415-97698-7 (Softcover)
International Standard Book Number-13: 978-0-415-97697-8 (Hardcover) 978-0-415-97698-7 (Softcover)
Library of Congress Card Number 2005036480

Library of Congress Cataloging-in-Publication Data

Stohrer, Sharon, 1955-
   The singer's companion / by Sharon Stohrer.
      p. cm.
   Includes bibliographical references (p.) and index.
   ISBN 0-415-97697-9 (hardback : alk. paper) -- ISBN 0-415-97698-7 (pbk. : alk. paper)
   1. Singing--Instruction and study. 2. Singing--Vocational guidance. I. Title.

MT820.S856 2006
783--dc22   2005036480

Taylor & Francis Group
is the Academic Division of Informa plc.

Visit the Taylor & Francis Web site at
http://www.taylorandfrancis.com

and the Routledge Web site at
http://www.routledge-ny.com

To My Students:
Past, Present, and Future

CONTENTS

PREFACE

Learning to sing is similar to taking a journey: there are ups and downs, challenges to face, pitfalls to avoid and abundant rewards that await those who persevere. *The Singer's Companion* can be your guide on that journey—informing your practice time, reiterating concepts your teacher has introduced, helping you make choices in your daily life that aid your growth as a singer. Whether your goal in taking lessons is to be accepted into a good choral group or sing well at a friend's wedding, or you plan to knock 'em dead one day at the Met or on Broadway, there is a wealth of information beyond the voice lesson that can speed your vocal, musical, and interpretive growth.

This book has grown out of years of teaching voice lessons, performance classes, opera workshops, and courses in vocal pedagogy and lyric diction. It began as studio letters written for students on several topics along with syllabi and course handouts. Those documents were later modified into magazine and journal articles and, finally, expanded and revised into book form. It is intended as a true companion, a source to consult for guidance and support as you embark on this journey.

ACKNOWLEDGMENTS

Many people helped in reading and preparing this book. First, thanks to my ever-patient editor, Richard Carlin and his equally patient colleagues. For preparation of musical examples, Steven "Maestro" Lott has my deepest appreciation. I am also grateful to my New York University student, Jenna Battipaglia, for allowing me to reproduce her practice/lesson log as a model. For general support, encouragement, and editorial help, thanks go to my loving husband, David Rives, and to Larry Alexander, Cristy Chory, Michael Clement, John Crowe, Diane and Ted Cushing, Susan Hermance Fedak, Stefanie Izzo, Barbara Paul, Mary Paul, and Robert "Doc" White.

1

GETTING STARTED

HOW TO FIND A GOOD VOICE TEACHER

FINDING A GOOD VOICE TEACHER is not as mysterious or difficult as it may seem at first glance. It is similar to the process of finding a good tutor or hair stylist or car mechanic: ask around. If a friend is studying voice and you hear improvement in your friend's singing and he or she seems to like their teacher—that may be someone to check out. You might also attend theatrical productions, voice recitals, or oratorio concerts that feature soloists. When there are voices that strike you as particularly beautiful and expressive, try to discover the names of the singers' teachers. Local colleges, universities, and conservatories are all worth investigating, because many offer lessons for the general public given by faculty or graduate students. Do not necessarily rule out famous voice teachers, because they may enjoy working with beginning students. By the same token, contrary to what you will see in the publicity for most colleges and universities, many of the best teachers are not big time performers. Some high school music departments keep lists of good local voice teachers—it may be worth a phone call. Local music stores are also an excellent resource for finding a voice teacher who is right for you.

While searching, give some thought to the kind of teaching you most enjoy. There are various teaching styles, and some might suit you and your progress better than others. Are you shy and introverted, needing a gregarious personality to draw you out and encourage you? Are you a perfectionist, hard on yourself, in need of someone warm and reassuring? Or do you respond best to someone who demands a great deal and reserves praise for the greatest effort? It would be wise to find out about teaching style and personality when asking people for teacher recommendations.

Most voice teachers are hardworking, pleasant people with high standards of conduct—but not all. One of the difficulties in the singing profession is that the instrument—that is, the voice—is out of view and internal. Most of the muscles used cannot be seen and many of the coordinations involved in singing are involuntary and brought about by imagery and concepts. All of this lends a cloak of mysteriousness to singing behind which some people can hide. Many of those people can sing beautifully themselves but cannot explain how they sing to others. Their own performing career is over and they teach to have income and involvement. There are others who teach with just a modicum of vocal knowledge, unaware of the harm they may be causing. And there are true charlatans, waiting to profit from innocent people. So how do you avoid these people? There are several ways to check out a teacher and several signs of trouble that tell you to avoid him or her:

- Voice teachers who are members of the National Association of Teachers of Singing (NATS) must subscribe to a stringent code of ethics to be part of the organization. This does not guarantee that any given teacher is the one for you, but you can generally rest assured that NATS members will not engage in unethical behavior. You can look online at http://www.nats.org to read their code of ethics and to look for a teacher in your area.
- Voice teachers who are members of an academic community are also usually reliable. Unethical behavior does occur on campuses, but it is less likely than in the private studio.
- There are several Web sites worth visiting: http://www.private lessons.com; http://www.voiceteacher.com; http://www.classical singer.com; and so forth. However, their service is informational only—they make no claim about the instructors' backgrounds or ethics.
- Generally, well-established teachers will be happy to spend a few minutes on the telephone with you answering your questions and explaining their approach. Often they will give a discounted or free initial consultation: a meeting to get acquainted, talk about goals and approaches, and have a mini-lesson. If the teacher you contact requires full payment for an initial lesson, that is no cause for alarm. What may be alarming is if the teacher requires that you sign up for several lessons or a given period of time when you first meet.

Some teachers prefer that their students commit to several weeks or months and pay in advance. That is fine, once the two of you have met and decided that you work well together. Most worthwhile teachers will allow you to take an initial lesson while considering other teachers as well. The teacher should also be willing to give you a few names of current students along with contact information. Checking these references can be invaluable. Any reputable teacher will also be happy to talk about his or her own vocal background, including degrees earned and performance credits.

- Red flags can include teachers whose main selling point is that they have a recording studio and can help you make recordings and become famous, as well as people who gush about how talented you are and how they are certain they can make a career or a recording contract happen for you. Even the best voices take time to fully develop and *no one* can guarantee a contract or career. Avoid teachers who say that you must study with them, that they are the only ones who can help you, and want you to stay away from any other teachers or coaches. Lastly, steer clear of teachers who promise that if you study with them, they will help you get auditions for agents or other contacts. When you run into such a person, thank them for their time, and be on your way.

In calling for information on voice lessons, be honest about your goals and needs. If you want just a few months of lessons to prepare for an audition for a local community chorale, say so. Some teachers are fine with helping beginners with short-term goals. Others prefer to fill their studios with students who plan to study for at least a year or two.

Be sure to find out what the teacher's fee is, whether the preference is for monthly payment (after an initial consultation), and whether there is an accompanist's fee. Also ask about the teacher's cancellation policy.

You may find the right teacher for you at the first consultation or lesson. Or you may need to have several such meetings before a good match is found between teacher and student. Be patient and start the process early if you have auditions or other deadlines coming up. Some singers stay with one teacher their entire lives, others change frequently. For musical theatre and other popular styles of singing, you might find a teacher who can help you in both building a solid classical (legit) technique and in learning styles and techniques appropriate to popular music. This is often not the case, so many singers begin by working on classical technique for several years and then find a teacher who specializes in contemporary techniques.

WHAT GOES ON IN A VOICE LESSON?

At my first voice lesson I was absolutely flabbergasted! Accustomed to choral singing and conductors' quick fixes, I assumed that gimmicks and tips would be the bulk of vocal training and I was totally unprepared for the natural, unfolding process of learning to sing. I could read music and had studied piano for years, but even that did not prepare me for the complex and very physical nature of singing. Allow me to take you through a typical voice lesson:

Generally, teachers will start a new student's lesson by talking about posture and perhaps doing a few stretches. Usually this is followed by some breathing exercises. At this point, it would be wise to bring out recording equipment of some kind (audiocassette recorder, iPod and mic, etc.) and a notebook so that you can remember the exercises and repeat them in your practice sessions. After focusing on posture and breathing, it is time to warm up the voice. Most instructors begin with easy sighs or scales, to get the breath flowing. Then they add exercises to work on support, legato, agility, register blending, vowel unification, and range extension. Your teacher will most likely start you with just a few warm-ups and add others as time goes on. For any given purpose (e.g., support) there are many vocalizes and some may work better for you than others. Be sure to ask in what order you should practice the exercises because that may have technical implications. Your recording equipment will come in handy here and when you practice at home you might simply use material recorded during a voice lesson to warm-up.

After warming up the voice it is time to work on repertoire. Bring any solo vocal music you may have to your first lesson but be prepared to buy additional music. Students usually begin with simple, flowing pieces in English and Italian (see the next section of this chapter for suggestions). Inform your teacher if you are fluent in a language other than English. There are so many coordinations to learn, that it is best for the beginner to work within a known language. Italian is used for many reasons including purity of vowels and legato writing. Make sure you understand how to pronounce every word before you leave your lesson—ask your teacher to record the text for you. Also let your teacher know if you have auditions, performances, or other projects coming up, since those events may inform repertoire selection.

If your goal is musical theatre or some other popular style of music, you still might be asked to begin with classical selections. Contrary to some people's fears, getting a classical or legit technique will *not* necessarily make you sound like an opera singer in other styles. If it is based on sound principles of efficient voice production, it will give you a solid, healthy foundation upon which to build (see the next section of this chapter for more information on this process).

After choosing material, your teacher (or the accompanist) will play a section of the piece and then you might vocalize it on a vowel. That is when your teacher can continue to focus on the technical issues introduced in the warm-ups. The instructor may require you to continue with the song on just a vowel so that you can focus on and attend to correct posture, relaxed jaw, deep and silent breaths, active support, and forward-tracking resonance. Patience is a virtue in the first few weeks of vocal study. Often singers work on just two or three very simple selections in order to focus on all the aspects just named. That can be difficult if the singer is accustomed to learning and performing a great deal of music in a choir. Just remember that you are starting a whole new way of singing and that numerous muscles are learning several new activities.

Using your recorder will help in your vocal progress. We hear ourselves largely through bones conducting the sound back to our ears. In fact, some researchers say that as much as 75 percent of what we hear is through this bone conduction. Because it distorts the sound, you would be wise to record your lessons and your practice sessions and listen carefully to the recording at least twice so that you can begin to bridge the gap between how your singing sounds to you and how it sounds to the rest of the world. This will also free you to focus on how the singing feels. While we do have to use our ears in order to be on pitch, the more we use our kinesthetic knowledge, the better. Focusing on the sensations of singing helps us to avoid strain and to grow technically. Since singing uses muscle coordinations that are out of view and some that are involuntary, it is vital to be able to memorize sensations and movements, in order to replicate in your own practice what goes on in the lesson. For many people, one of the greatest challenges of voice training is learning to live in our bodies. If that is the case with you, be sure to read the section on "Process Oriented Practicing" in chapter 2 for tips on increasing body awareness.

Before you leave the lesson, discuss how often and how long to practice and how your teacher would like you to approach each piece. Your instructor will most likely set goals and expectations for the following lesson, but if not, then please ask. Be sure that you understand what is expected of you, that all the concepts presented make sense to you, and that you have no questions about the music or the diction. In subsequent lessons you will be guided into greater understanding of the music, finer use of vocal technique, and deeper commitment to artistry.

SUGGESTIONS REGARDING REPERTOIRE

Your teacher will most likely assign two or three simple, flowing songs in English and perhaps a piece or two in Italian. It is prudent for the beginner to sing pieces that lie primarily mid-voice, with occasional forays into higher or lower parts of the range. Over time the instructor can use vocalizes to extend the range, and then add some songs that require the singer to utilize those pitches.

There are some excellent collections of vocal music available. *Twenty-Six Italian Songs and Arias*, edited by John Glen Paton and published by Alfred comes in two volumes: medium high and medium low. Both include a CD of accompaniments, information on the composers, background of each song, and translations. A good book of limited range, American folk-style songs is *The Songs of John Jacob Niles* published by G. Schirmer. It is available in two volumes: low voice and high voice. Joan Frey Boytim has edited a series of fine volumes published by G. Schirmer. Collected by voice type, they begin with *Easy Songs for Beginning Singers*, next *The First Book of Solos, the First Book of Solos Part II*, and then a collection with more challenges, *The Second Book of Solos.* Each volume has several selections in English, Italian, French, German, and Spanish along with sacred repertoire, folk song settings, and spirituals.

It is vitally important to be on the cautious side when choosing repertoire. You are learning a very physical art that must unfold slowly and organically. Just as you would not expect a runner to begin training with a five-mile run, nor should you expect to tackle difficult repertoire for at least several months, more likely for years. I have heard amazing stories of young, inexperienced students being assigned heavy operatic arias such as "Un bel di" from Puccini's *Madam Butterfly* or "Vissi d'arte" from Puccini's *Tosca.* (That is certainly a red flag that either the student misunderstands expectations or the teacher is not the right one for beginners.) Those arias belong to the "verismo" style of opera, requiring large, mature voices and reliable, secure technique. In my opinion, most beginning students of all ages should focus on singing songs, with judicious use of lighter arias. After several years of study, often in collegiate training, they can begin adding arias and gradually progress to the heavier material in their upper class and graduate years. Occasionally, a voice that is of large operatic proportions might be given a mid-weight aria as a stretch piece. However, under most circumstances, singing heavy material early on can easily damage the voice, perhaps irreparably.

For some of the information below, I am most grateful to my New York University colleagues Dianna Heldman and Michael Ricciardone:

As mentioned previously, students interested in musical theatre and other popular genres would be well served by beginning with classical songs. When it is time to add some musical theatre repertoire, there are some wonderful anthologies available. Hal Leonard publishes a collection by voice type entitled *Musical Theatre Classics*. Each volume includes background information on the shows and a CD of accompaniments. Hal Leonard also publishes a series called *The Singer's Musical Theatre Anthology*. These volumes, edited by Richard Walters, are categorized by voice type and presented in their authentic settings. There are three volumes for each voice type and a book of duets. These two collections do not progress, as Boytim's classical volumes do, from easier to more challenging material. The teacher and student need to be selective and informed before settling on particular repertoire.

It is especially good for the singer's vocal development to begin the acquisition of musical theatre repertoire with songs written between 1940 and 1960, often referred to as "The Golden Age." Rodgers and Hammerstein, in particular, wrote songs whose melodies can be compared with those of early Fauré and Schubert. The songs are lyrical, midrange, not too lengthy, and the treatment of the text is sensitive. After some time working with such material, one can carefully, and with guidance, begin to add more recent songs.

Just as a classical singer should not attempt to sing verismo opera until the technique is secure, the young musical theatre singer should not attempt later material by Sondheim, Schwartz, and their contemporaries, but rather stay with earlier songs. Later works by these composers are similar in their vocal demands to verismo opera—especially the ranges and the dramatic weight of the music. Therefore, be judicious in adding songs by modern composers, ask for help from your teacher, and be patient until your technique is quite advanced.

The songs written today for musical theatre require a dependable technique. Women need to be able to negotiate freely and easily among head voice, chest, and mixed registers. Men need to be comfortable using the upper parts of their range, negotiating transitions with ease. This facility with registers can take some time to develop. When your teacher feels that you can attempt some of this repertoire, be mindful of the fact that the singers you hear in recordings are often much older and certainly much more experienced than you are. Avoid imitating them and sing this music with your own voice.

STEPS IN LEARNING A SONG OR ARIA

Perhaps the most important suggestion is to take your time in learning music so that you do not learn it incorrectly, because once mistakes are learned, it is nearly impossible to unlearn them. Try using all the steps listed below. As you become more expert in learning your songs, you may find that some steps can be eliminated in learning some pieces, and you may make modifications to the process. Depending on the difficulty of the piece, this process may take a few hours or several days.

Enjoy the poetry of the song or the text of the aria. Especially if it is in older English or a foreign language, practice speaking it until it falls easily off the tongue. When it is in a foreign language, it is vital that you add a translation step to this process. Writing out the translation word-for-word on the sheet music will help you to be aware of the important words as you learn and sing the song, and help you to make convincing stresses on those important words. Find a place where you can feel alone and uninhibited and practice saying the text as if speaking with a friend, then as if giving a poetry reading to a small group, then as if orating on stage in a large theatre. Have fun with it and act it out, if you like. The emotional connection will go a long way to help you learn, memorize, and internalize the piece.

Find a way to learn the rhythm of the song. If you learn music from recorded lessons or commercial recordings, use this step in the process to get a solid rhythmical foundation: tap the rhythmic pattern of your vocal line or clap it. When you have more advanced skills, you might tap a foot to the underlying meter and clap out your rhythmical pattern. Be certain to spend quality time on this step of the process. Unlike most instrumentalists, singers often have problems with rhythm, falsely believing that the natural rhythm of the words will keep them on track, or that the accompaniment will carry them along. In addition to learning vocal technique, it is vital to pay particular attention to rhythm in order to be a prepared, independent musician.

Put text and rhythm together. Perhaps tap a foot to keep the meter going or use a metronome. You might try it several times at different speeds. Once that feels comfortable, chant the song on one pitch. This will do a lot to assure rhythmic accuracy. See if you can do it expressively, paying attention to dynamics and chanting in a legato line.

Learn the melody by playing it on an instrument or using solfege syllables. Then sing the melody on a vowel ("ah" or "aw" are good), paying close attention to your technique, and aiming for a smooth, moving, expressive line. Try this at several different speeds. It is generally a good idea to sing a given song or aria on a vowel for several days or weeks (see chapter 2, "Practicing"). Nevertheless, you are probably anxious by now to hear how it all works together, so sing the piece through. Now you are at the point of bringing this newly learned music to your voice lesson.

As you continue to work on the piece and attempt to incorporate all that your teacher suggests, it is also helpful to find ways to relate to the piece on a personal level. This stage can include analyzing the music, text, and elements of drama as discussed in chapter 3, "Working with the Score." It can also be helpful to physicalize it by hearing the music in your head and dancing in a free-form dance, or bowing an imaginary violin or cello, or conducting it.

Use your imagination to have fun with your newly learned piece. Maybe one of the following silly ideas will appeal to your funny bone. It is often astounding how much this playful approach helps one to really know and intimately understand the piece, and how that greatly improves one's actual performance:

- Sing it very strictly, with no emotion and then as over-the-top emotional/hammy as possible.
- Make index cards of strong emotions (mourning, rage, terror, etc.) and randomly select one while singing. Perhaps sing the whole piece that way or take a new card every few phrases. See if one emotion really helps in the singing more than others.
- Sing it as if you were a little whiney child and then as if you were a very famous opera singer.
- Sing it in another style: rock, country, folk, etc.
- Sing it as you really want it to sound—your ideal concept.

2

PRACTICING

PRACTICE IS VITAL TO PROGRESS. It truly is that simple. Without regular practice, a singer may make some technical gains, but with regular practice that same singer's technique will surely grow in a strong and steady fashion. Singing is, after all, a physical activity and the process of acquiring technique is an organic one, built on repetition. Just as you would not expect to progress in soccer or basketball without regular individual and team practices, neither should you expect to make gains in range and freedom and flexibility without consistent, thoughtful practice. Singers are both the instrument and the player and that instrument is best maintained by regular use. The player, the musician, the artist also needs nurturing, since beautiful singing is not only making the right sounds in the right songs. To be an artist, one must both master the songs' challenges and know them intimately. In other words, your work is not simply to learn notes and rhythms, breathing and placement, but to also know the pieces as well as if you had written them, and to perform them convincingly. Activities designed to foster musicianship and artistry are listed below and in chapter 3, "Working with the Score."

In addition to balancing being the instrument and the player, we must also use both body awareness and analytical thought in singing. Normally in performance the body awareness is paramount, with some assistance from analytical thought. Practice, however, is an excellent time to use analysis—why some approaches work better than others, what the next step in learning this song should be, and what different methods could be used to gain greater freedom in a particular passage. Remember that mindless practicing, singing things over and over with no purpose in sight, is a waste of time. Thus, in balancing mind and body, instrument and player, let us now consider practicing in a step-by-step way.

HOW TO PRACTICE

The first question to ask is what kind of daily regimen should you have.

The Daily Regimen

- Sing when you are fresh and awake—preferably late morning or early afternoon. If it is morning, be sure that your practice time is at least two hours after arising. Warm up carefully and adequately before you sing in classes and rehearsals. You would not expect a dancer to just go on stage and start twirling and jumping without adequate physical warm up. The same is true for singing. You will avoid injury and strain and you will have greater longevity as a singer if you ease your voice into production each day.
- Do some gentle stretches before you sing. Our bodies are our instruments and they need to be tuned. Eat a light meal before you sing, for the chewing and swallowing help warm up and loosen the same muscles that are used for singing.
- Warm up slowly and carefully, looking for the correct coordination rather than a beautiful sound. Be patient with yourself. Come back to it later on if your voice is not responding. Do not push yourself! When your voice refuses to cooperate, take a day off and study your music. Oftentimes a difficult singing day is a clue that you need more rest or that you are on the verge of illness. Be kind to yourself.
- It is best to use the exercises your teacher has introduced in lessons. If, however, you would occasionally like to vary the approach, see the final section of this chapter for a series of warm-ups.
- It can be overwhelming at first to remember all the different aspects of good singing, including: correct posture, free and forward articulation, relaxed jaw, breathing that is calm and low, adequate support, and tone that is resonant and free. One way to train yourself in these or any other technical matters is to pay attention to one at a time as you repeat a warm-up exercise. You might sing a scale focusing on your low breaths, and then watch yourself in a mirror during the next repetition to be sure that your jaw is released, and so forth. After some time, most of these aspects will be at your command most of the time.
- When you can, alternate singing with other activities. For example, spend about twenty minutes in gentle warm-ups then do something else for a while. Do a few stretches and one more exercise then practice repertoire for thirty to sixty minutes, but no more than that. Some instrumentalists can practice for several hours at a

time. For singers, after an hour or so we begin to reach the point of diminishing returns. It is better for your technique and your overall vocal health to stop before your voice feels tired.

- In all your practicing, no matter what else you are doing, keep a part of your mind focused on being aware of what is going on in your body. The more that you live in your body this way while singing, the more integrated your singing will be and the quicker you will be to catch any strain. Your ability to focus will also improve.
- Practice five to six days a week and be certain to take a day off. Like training muscles for athletics, your body will better absorb the new coordinations you are learning if given some downtime.

How Should You Practice?

- Vary the session: chant the words in rhythm to one song, sing another on AH, work with another on the vowels of the words.
- Make a practice plan so that you accomplish your goals over the course of several days or weeks. During your practice time, take frequent short breaks to rest.
- Keep a journal while you practice. That will help you remember questions, sensations, breakthroughs while they are fresh and will force you to take minibreaks. Below are a few pages from the practice log of one of my students at New York University. Note how she lists in order what she does in her practice session and what insights, breakthroughs, or problems present themselves. We start our lessons by reviewing this journal and it then informs us what we will do in the lesson. What a valuable, time-saving device this is! It also firmly plants the student in the driver's seat, helping to foster independence. While it is important for all singers to check in with a teacher from time to time, the eventual goal of voice lessons is an independent, self-directed singing artist.
- Occasionally give yourself a silent practice session. Play a recording of yourself singing and lip-sync, paying attention to facial and body expression, to your focus and to breathing. Do this in front of a mirror, if possible.
- Use your own emotional state and your acting skills to spice up the session. If you are intensely angry one day, sing everything in an angry way. You may find that other emotions emerge and that you gain some useful insights into your body energy as well as a good catharsis. Try playing different characters for different songs. You might even use various emotions on the same line of a song and see what feels best. Experiment and enjoy!

- Occasionally, use your practice time as a "mock performance." Sing through your pieces without stopping, using all the stagecraft and interpretive skills you would use in a real performance situation. Record yourself and listen carefully later. We so often just go through the motions when we practice. Turning that session into a performance increases energy and communication and prepares us in many subtle ways for the real thing.

Lesson Log—Monday, March 21, 2005

"Simple Little Things"
Introduction—more "head voice-y"
"Dreams"—sing it often—remember not to get stuck on the word.
Verse—speak more, and sing it away from yourself.
"Summertime"
Slide
Don't overpronounce words
Breathe in the starting notes
"What's the Use of Wonderin'?"
Your "oo" sounds "French" sometimes!
Don't start words with an "H" in front of them.
"Ten Minutes Ago"
"Sing more"
Lift through eyes.
*Remember: posture!—Don't cave in.

For Next Time:
Jury Songs—

1. "I'll Know"
2. "Summertime"
3. "The Salley Gardens"
4. "Simple Little Things"
5. "What's the Use of Wonderin'?"
6. "When I Have Sung My Songs"
* "Ten Minutes Ago"

Practice Log—Tuesday, March 22, 2005

Warm-ups
Lip-trills—starting on A below Middle C, ascending and descending
5 note scales to A above High C.

-OO-AH-OO and EE-AH-EE in the same pattern as above.

Descending sighs on AH from G above High C, down to E above Middle C.

"Summertime"

Sang on "AH"—twice

"Breathe in" first notes

Slide and don't overpronounce!

Sang with words— three times

Have to remember not to pronounce ends of words, especially!

"Simple Little Things"

Sang with words—three times

Have to remember to keep the song, especially the introduction, in Head Voice!

Keep the whole song "simpler."

Practice Log: Wednesday, March 23, 2005

Warm-ups

Lip-trills—starting on A below Middle C, ascending and descending five-note scales to A above High C.

-OO-AH-OO and EE-AH-EE in the same pattern as above.

Descending sighs on AH from G above High C, down to E above Middle C.

"Ma made me go, too" descending from G above High C

"I'll Know"

Sang on a vowel (AH)—twice

"Breathe in" starting notes

Sang with words—three times

Remember to sing each phrase in a line away from you

Sing through eyes!

"I'll be strong!"—STRAW (ng)

"When I Have Sung My Songs"

Sang on vowels (AH-OO)—twice

Release!

Sang with words—three times

Sing through eyes, and move forward through each phrase.

Think more operatic! Keep vibrato spinning.

*I sang this while moving my arms in a circular motion. It helped me keep vibrato "spinning."

While holding out "loved" or "sing," keep off consonants/stay on the vowel!

Practice Log: Thursday, March 24, 2005

Warm-ups

Lip-trills—starting on A below Middle C, ascending and descending five-note scales to A above High C.

-OO-AH-OO and EE-AH-EE in the same pattern as above.

Chest voice to head voice exercise—starting on A below Middle C, on "AH" (A,B,C#-3 times in chest and descending triad in head voice.)

A few Sirens!

"The Salley Gardens"

Sang alternating the vowels AH and OO—twice

Keep vibrato spinning and release!

Sang with words—three times

Don't overpronounce words and stay on vowels more.

p.3, second system—"as the grass grows on the weirs"—keep light and spinning forward. Don't think about getting all the words out.

"Ten Minutes Ago"

Sang with words—four times

Head voice—lies in my break and mix. Don't push!

*Remember: this is a waltz!

Danced a few measures—getting it in my body really helps me with the tempo of this song.

p. 2, third system—"taking me back to the skies!"—"SKAH(s)" The "ies"/eyes is distracting me and making my voice fall back into the wrong place.

Practice Log: Friday, March 25, 2005

Warm-ups

(Already warmed up)

Quick "refresher"

Lip-trills—A below Middle C to A above High C (scales, ascending and descending.)

Sirens!

"What's the Use of Wonderin'?"

Sang on the vowels EE and AH —twice

Sang with words—three times

 "Or if you like the way he wears his hat" and every other phrase like that, needs to start from above! On the last note of the phrase, remember to just stay on the vowel! (Those are my most troubled parts of this song.)

"Summertime"

Sang on the vowel AH —twice

This song is OK when I sing it on a vowel.

Sang with words—three times

The words complicate my singing in this song!

Every note held out (and every high note) can be underpronounced and just sung on the vowel!

Keep vibrato spinning and all phrases connected in a line moving forward.

*I spun my arms so much during this song (in order to release vibrato) that my arms are very tired! —But it worked!

Saturday, March 26, 2005

Review Day!

Warm-ups

Lip-trills—starting on A below Middle C, ascending and descending five-note scales to A above High C.

-OO-AH-OO and EE-AH-EE in the same pattern as above.

Sirens!

"Ma made me go, too" descending from G above High C

Descending sighs on AH from G above High C, down to E above Middle C.

"Ten Minutes Ago"

Sang with words —twice

Waltz!

Head voice!

*I didn't look at the music, mostly, and it sounded better because I thought a lot less and the song came out to be more what it should be!

"The Salley Gardens"

Sang with words—twice

"Breathe in" each starting note, release, and keep it forward moving

*The High A is getting better—I need to remember to think before starting those phrases.

"I'll Know"

Sang with words —once (I love this song!)

"Breathing in" the first notes of each phrase and staying on the vowels really helps a lot during this song.

"When I Have Sung My Songs"

Sang with words—twice

Operatic and forward

Last page "Never! Never sing again"—very open and bright. I love that part.

"Simple Little Things"
Sang with words —twice
Not so "simple" to sing correctly!
*I think I get too caught up in how pretty this song is and I get distracted
from my technique because I listen to myself.
Much better, though. My head voice was there the whole time.
"What's the Use of Wonderin'?"
Sang with words—twice
*On my troubling phrases I am really trying to lighten up, approach
it from above, and sing on the vowels of the last words. When I do
all of that, they are very easy to sing.

What to Do if You Are too Tired or Sick to Practice or Your Voice is Overworked?

There is a great deal to do. Ideally, the activities listed below will become
a regular and important part of your total preparation.

- Write out all the words of your songs on note cards and carry them
  with you. Say the words aloud, in your head, write them out several
  times.
- Listen to recordings of your songs—several versions, different artists,
  and different conductors; listen with the score and without. Begin to
  absorb the subtle nuances that make for artistry. Ask yourself "How
  did the singer get that effect? Can I sound as excited/sad/angry in
  this song as she or he does?"
- When your piece is in another language or older English, write out
  the text in your own words. You will own the piece this way, with a
  subtle but noticeable improvement in your interpretation.
- When you are working on an aria or a show tune, listen to a recording of the *entire* opera or show. Learn why your character sings the
  piece, to whom and when.

PROCESS-ORIENTED PRACTICING

Do you wake up in the morning thinking, "When can I practice today?"
Do you make that hour the highest priority of the day, scheduling it
during the time that you are most alert and energetic? Is it a fun activity
that you anticipate with pleasure? With some experimentation and with
experience, the practice session can become fulfilling in itself, a time for
a bit of self-indulgence and a respite from all the tasks and worries of
daily life.

It can be a challenge to remain in the moment while practicing, especially if a recital is coming up or you are in a show or other pressures make you feel that you need to accomplish certain goals in a given period of time. That is, however, exactly what we all need to do: keep our practice process oriented rather than product oriented. Then we usually make the most progress and avoid using poor technique to achieve a given effect. Some suggestions follow to help you in this process.

Get yourself good recording equipment. *Recording your practice sessions is invaluable.* Then, you can turn off the critic—the voice that is listening for tone, pitch, diction, and line—and, instead, focus on your coordinations and on the sensations of singing. Later you can put on the critic's ears when you listen to the recording, and make notes in your scores. In fact, some of the best learning happens while studying scores: follow the music in real time (do not rush through) and breathe where you would actually breathe. See if you can actually hear it or have the body sensations as if you were about to sing (Eloise Ristad calls this "muscle memory in reverse" in her book *A Soprano on Her Head*). Go ahead and take pauses to make notes of insights. If you faithfully study your scores as an activity in itself and as part of listening to your recordings, you will be able to integrate more quickly and fully the changes you desire. Then when you go to practice, more of your focus can be on performing and the actual pleasure of making music.

As often as possible, practice in front of a mirror. In our culture, it can be difficult for all of us, but especially women, to turn off the appearance critic—we all want to be thinner or taller or prettier or something and we avoid mirrors for that very reason. Yet once again, as with a recorder, the mirror can be your best teacher. When you can hush those critical appearance judges by attending to the task at hand, the mirror can free you to focus in on sensations because you can clearly see if your posture is off or your jaw is tense, and your brain does not have to think about those things. Some people are helped in this by using two mirrors: a full-length one and a hand-held mirror. It seems to bypass the appearance critic because of the double image—it is as if we were watching someone else.

Warm up slowly and carefully, looking for the correct coordinations, rather than listening for tone. It is an excellent idea to do some body stretches and a breathing exercise or two before beginning the warm-up. If you have studied Yoga, some excellent postures to help expand the body for singing and quiet the mind are: woodchopper (Ardha Chakrasana), triangle (Trikonasana), head of the cow (Gomukhasana), and dancer's posture (Natarajasana).

Develop your own routine for turning off extraneous thoughts and focusing on singing. Maybe the stretches and warm-ups alone will get you in the moment or you might need your journal to write down all your worries and concerns or make lists of other things you need to do. Oftentimes making a practice plan ahead of time can help you focus on what needs attention in that practice session and not think about all the other songs or challenges facing you. It might help to listen for a few minutes to a favorite singer and allow the beauty to transport you to a more physical, emotive, intuitive place. Some singers like to begin by lying on their backs with knees raised and feet flat on the floor. They take deep breaths and release all their cares and worries in sighs, eventually adding tone to the airflow.

While you are singing, both warm-ups and literature, keep checking your body for tension and release as much as possible. Is your throat as open and relaxed as if you were drinking a tumbler of water? Is your jaw hanging—not tight or pushed down? Are you tracking resonance in a free and forward manner? Is your sternum high and is your body expanded? Are your breaths silent? If you have studied Alexander Technique, you can use those directions ("Let my neck be free, to let my head come slightly forward," etc.) as you sing. Ideally, you should leave a practice session with your throat feeling as fresh as if it had not been used at all. Be vigilant for tension and release it before it becomes pain or discomfort.

In order to be concerned with how the singing feels, it is vital that you avoid using text when learning your music. Staying on a vowel for a few *weeks* will help you attend to your coordinations (matters of support, resonance-tracking, and so forth) and avoid tensions. Look on your practice time as an experiment and be inventive: if high pitches are uncomfortable, try them down an octave; if a held note feels tight, try pulsing it or just touching it and going on, then gradually increasing the time. Use lip-trills, open-mouth hums, or whatever is loose for getting rapid passages in your body.

In every stage of learning a piece, search for ways to engage your right brain (imagery and sensory awareness) in the process. For example, as you are singing some phrases on "AH," imagine that your feet are breathing or that your whole body is breathing in and out. Or imagine that your entire body is singing or that you are dancing to the music through your voice. This use of the right hemisphere in practice will help trigger it to take a greater role in performance, bringing greater relaxation.

If you find it challenging to live in your body while training your voice you might try some remedies to increase your kinesthetic awareness. Take some Yoga classes, dance lessons, or Alexander Technique lessons, or try a few sessions of Tai Chi. You might also experiment with free-form dancing to a particular phrase, and then attempt to keep that level of muscle awareness while you sing the same phrase. During a of limited range, you could even sing while dancing. If you kn primary mode of learning is visual, try practicing with your Maybe sing a phrase or two with closed eyes and then repea eyes, trying to keep the same level of body awareness. If your primary mode of learning is auditory, try singing with headphones on. You might also benefit from closing your eyes (see chapter 6 "A Few Words about Technique" for more information on learning modalities). Some people find it helpful to lie on their backs with knees raised and feet flat on the floor. In this position, it is easier to feel what is going on in your body while you sigh deeply and sing some easy phrases of limited range. Later you might stand and see if you can replicate the body awareness gained while lying down or you might try some deep sighs or easy phrases while seated. In trying any of these ideas, please slow down and consider this growth in kinesthetic awareness the goal for your practice. You would certainly hinder this process by expecting yourself to learn several pieces or attain great technical growth during these sessions.

Occasionally use your practice session as a purely meditative time. Tune into the body sensations involved in singing, to what you are feeling, to the actual vibrations of sound. Developing this kind of awareness brings with it an ability to focus that helps most performers overcome any distractions or jitters. Remember why you first came to love music in general and singing in particular. Revel in the sensations and allow yourself to fully savor and enjoy the sounds. Giving yourself the indulgence of a meditative session can be a reward of sorts and certainly a break from all the responsibilities and the to-do lists in your busy life. Enjoy!

A Sample Sequence of Exercises for Vocal Warm-up

Start with breathing exercises and then something that gets the breath flowing while singing. Next, add exercises to work on support, agility, legato, register blending, and vowel unification. Listed below are three exercises for these areas of technique. It is typically best to choose one from each area, but follow your teacher's advice.

Breathing
1. Breathe in for the count of two, hold for four to practice the suspension we need in singing, and then hiss the air out for the count of eight. (Rather than hiss, you could resist the airflow by pursing your lips and blowing out as if through a drinking straw.) Keep the inhalation at the count of two, but increase the others as you repeat.

2. To practice taking quick, low breaths, first tighten your stomach muscles slightly. Then exhale all your air. Only when you have exhaled every last molecule of air, breathe in. You will undoubtedly find the air rushing in your body and discover a very low place for inhalation.

3. Most of the time we want to avoid tanking up because it can actually produce some tension. Yet there are occasional passages that require enormous amounts of breath. To practice for this and increase your lung capacity, try this yogic breathing technique. As if you were building a stack of golden coins, start your breathing very low in your body—starting at the pelvic floor—releasing your lower abdomen. Continue to breathe, building a column of air until you feel completely full of air up to your collarbone. Hold for a moment or two and then exhale to reverse the process.

Breath Flowing

1. Start with easy, airy sighs on AH: 5-1. Begin in your midrange and go up by half-steps and then down. Avoid going very high or low—just a comfortable, easy start to singing. You might want to vary this by alternating EE and AH in the sighs.

2. Continue the sigh feeling, staying in a comfortable range, but now moving the voice on 5-3-4-2-3-1-2-7-1. Take this pattern up by half steps and then down by half steps, letting the piano and your brain do the articulating for you, and just continuing the feeling of a sigh. Again, you might want to occasionally vary the vowel.

3. Instead of sighs, try lip-trilling five-tone scales, starting in your low range and moving up by half steps. Don't go too high.

Support

1. Slide on AH 1-5-1-8-1, resisting *before* you go to the 5th and the octave. Let the pitches feel as if they fly up out of low, grounded support. You might alternate with other vowels, but be sure to keep the throat open and the work going on in your support muscles. Start relatively low in your range and go up and then down by half steps. This exercise could be taken a little lower and a little higher than the previous three.

2. In addition to, or instead of, the exercise above, you might do some staccato arpeggios on various vowels. Placing your hands just under your ribcage, make those muscles work against your hands as you sing 1-3-5-8-5-3-1, starting low in your range and going

    first up and then down by half-steps. Staccato exercises can be a great way to extend the upper range, since the singer just "touches" the note.

3. Once you have worked on some upper-range arpeggios for a few weeks, you might elongate the exercise above to 1-3-5-8-8-8-8-5-3-1.

Agility

1. Now, move your voice in nine-tone scales, starting in midrange and moving first up and then down by half steps. You can do the scales on a lip-trill, on various vowels, or even start with a lip-trill and then see if you can place a vowel as forward and free as the lip-trill by about the third note of the scale.

2. For agility, releasing the voice and allowing the vibrato to emerge, sing the following exercise on AH or AW. It may help to feel as if you were laughing while singing. Keep the exercise moving. Go up and down by half steps, as low and as high as you can comfortably go.

3. Sing this exercise detached and rapidly, gently moving your head and neck to avoid any tension and experiment with various vowels and dynamics. Keep this one at midrange. 1-2-3-4-5-5-5-5-5-4-3-2-1.

Legato

1. For an exercise to work on constant motion, constant spin, constant legato, try the following on AH, moving throughout your range, making sure that you keep the motion going through each note, whether it is of shorter or longer value.

2. In this exercise, alternate detaching each note and then keeping that kind of energy in the next repetition, while singing as legato and smoothly as possible. This would be good to start midrange and go as high you can comfortably go. Use AW as your vowel.

3. You might also try simply sliding 1-8-1 on any vowel and then singing an octave scale, seeing if you can keep the feel of the slide underneath. Start midrange and go up and down by half steps, seeing how high and low is comfortable.

Ah_____   Ah_____

Register Blending

1. For women, find head voice around F top of the staff on OO—making a babylike sound on descending 5-1 slides. Go up to A above the staff. Then, like a petulant child, whine "ma made me go, too" (the 5 vowels) on a descending five-tone scale starting on the F at the top of the staff. Carry this down to A below MC, attempting to whine the entire time. It will go a great distance towards blending all the registers.

2. For men, do a few five-tone scales on OO in falsetto. Then, starting around A above middle C, do octave slides on AH from falsetto down. It will help if you keep the lower tone a bit soft, or think of it as in front of you, or imagine you are singing away from yourself. As you descend, you will eventually yodel, but as you continue to practice this exercise, the yodel will get lower and lower. This exercise will help with register blending and with ease in head voice.

3. For both sexes, try the following starting in head voice, comfortably high, and taking it down into chest register by half steps. Use the vowel EE and aim to keep all the descending notes feeling as if they were staying in the same resonance level as the first note—it can help to feel as if you were singing away from yourself or singing in front of yourself. 5-4-5-3-5-2-5-1.

Ee_____

Vowel Matching (Do these midrange until they are mastered, then try higher and lower in your range.)

1. Alternate the sequence starting on EE and then on OO. The goal is to track the forward resonance of the EE vowel in all the other vowels and the open throat comfort of the OO vowel in all the other vowels.

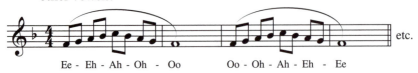

etc.

Ee - Eh - Ah - Oh - Oo   Oo - Oh - Ah - Eh - Ee

2. To help match EE and AH in comfort and resonance, try singing hung-EE, hung-AH, down a five-tone scale. Place both vowels right where you feel the buzz from the "ng" of hung.

etc.

Hung-ee Hung-ah Hung-ee Hung-ah   Hung-ee ___

3. Another exercise to match EE and AH in comfort and resonance is to simply sing a five-tone scale 1-1-2-2-3-3-4-4-5-5-4-4-3-3-2-2-1-1 in midrange, going up and down by half steps. Let just the tongue make the difference between EE and AH.

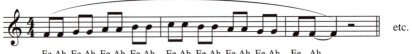

etc.

Ee-Ah Ee-Ah Ee-Ah Ee-Ah   Ee-Ah Ee-Ah Ee-Ah Ee-Ah   Ee Ah ___

3

WORKING WITH THE SCORE

There are several reasons for spending some time studying your music in depth. Your sense of the composer's intentions will grow, as will your awareness of the music's tensions, climaxes, momentum, and so forth. By intimately understanding how the music unfolds, your performance of it cannot help but improve in many subtle ways. You will also be better equipped to accurately and concisely describe to your accompanist your interpretation of the work and where he or she needs to follow your lead, support the voice more, set the mood, and so on. Knowing the composition well makes memorization much easier. In fact, if you take the time to thoroughly understand text, music, and drama, you may find that you have memorized the piece without even trying.

ANALYZING VOCAL MUSIC

Along with practicing, listening to recordings, attending concerts, and participating in workshops and performances, analyzing your music is an important element of performance preparation. Many kinds of analyses can be made, from an actual harmonic or structural analysis to character development.

Just as there are several reasons to analyze, there are various ways to study the music and text. First, write out the translation word-for-word. Use a good dictionary, books that give such translations, or consult with a native speaker. (Unfortunately, most online translation helps are inaccurate for poetic language.) Practice saying the awkward-sounding translation until it makes sense to you. Be sure to indicate in your score the most important words. When the text is in older English, write it out in your own words and practice saying this. Spend time speaking the original text as well, so that it falls easily off your tongue and you incorporate the natural stresses of the language.

If you have taken theory and analysis classes, do a complete harmonic analysis of your piece. Perhaps this could be an extra-credit assignment for class? In any case, ask your theory instructor to check over your work.

You might compare analyses. A very famous song or aria would have several analyses and other kinds of reviews in books and periodicals. It may be considered from viewpoints of form, diction, drama and interpretation. Look for contradictions and see if you agree with the authors.

Whatever work you do on further understanding your pieces will be of value. If you make a little time everyday for such activity, the work will settle in your mind, and your own creative ideas will grow.

Below are two forms: one for analyzing a song, the other for an aria. Both are self-explanatory and lead you into looking closely at the accompaniment, understanding the character and his or her motivations, and discovering how the music determines interpretation.

Song Analysis Form: Overview

1. Review the poem as a piece of literature; make any comments here. Include whether the poem is part of a cycle or has any special meaning to the composer.
2. What is the story, what facts are you *given*?
3. What underlying emotions or images are *implied* by the words?
4. What ideas/images/facts are suggested by the music? What is the composer's interpretation of the poem?
5. Why do you think the composer chose this key, meter, and form?

Song Analysis Study: Accompaniment Study

1. Is the accompaniment intended to be an equal partner or a literal accompaniment? If the voices are equal, who is soloist when?
2. How does the accompaniment help create the mood? Does it describe an underlying element (such as the spinning wheel in Schubert's "Gretchen am Spinnrade") or does it word-paint or reflect the scene?
3. Does it always change when the vocal part does? Anticipates? Follows?
4. What part of the song's deepest meaning is expressed by the accompaniment?

Song Analysis Study: Character and Scene Sketch

If a narrator speaks, why does she or he tell the story?

If a narrator speaks, how does she or he feel about the situation, events, and outcome?

If a character speaks, who am I?

Where am I? What surrounds me? Does the setting change in the course of the song?

What time is it? (century, year, season, day, hour)

What happened before I spoke?

To whom do I speak? (describe) Is that person/object present?

What is my objective (what I want) and obstacle (what is in the way)?

Any places in the vocal line or accompaniment that suggest change of stance, gestures, change of focus?

Aria Analysis: Before Commencing Analysis

Listen to the entire opera with a score or libretto, concentrating on text and plot and character. Listen to the entire opera without a score or libretto to absorb the singers' artistry, the sweep of the work, and the many facets that make for beauty. (This kind of analysis can also work for musical theatre repertoire.)

Read the entire libretto, noting what the character says about him- or herself and what others say about the character.

Note what biographical information is given in the libretto. When areas are blank, be creative in inventing a thorough biography and make the character come alive to you. What are the character's favorite colors, foods, and hobbies? What is the character's family like? Use aspects of your own background and personality, if applicable.

Give careful thought to deciding what the motivation is. It may be obvious or you might need to consider three possibilities and live with them for a while. Pare it down to an infinitive verb, such as "to woo," "to reveal," "to vindicate," and so forth.

OPERA   **CHARACTER**
ACT & SCENE   **ARIA TITLE**

General Comments

Character

Age, occupation, status (maid = low status, queen = high, etc.)

Background (include family)

What do I say about myself?

What do other characters in the opera say about me?

What does my language say about me? (blunt, poetic, evasive, etc.)

Physical attributes (handicaps, remarkable features or hair color, etc.):

What is my personality like?

Where do I live and move from? (e.g., head, heart, groin, solar plexus)

What is my speed? Do I move and talk quickly, deliberately, slowly?

How do I move? Does dress influence the movement?

Atmosphere

What time is it? (century, year, season, day, hour)

Where am I? (which country, rural or urban, building, room, area of room)

What surrounds me?

What just happened prior to the aria?

Motivation

What is this aria's objective (what I want) and obstacle (what is in the way)?

What do I do to get what I want?

What is my through-line? (my overall objective through the course of the opera)

Music

What does the music say about me?

Any clues to alterations of thought/mood in this aria through changes of orchestration, tempo, dynamics, rubato, high notes?

Are there places where the orchestral music or the vocal line itself suggests movements or gestures?

WITHOUT THE SCORE: TIPS FOR MEMORIZING

Once we fully understand the score with all its complexities, then it is time to get away from the printed page. Singers generally perform from memory. For some this is simple; others struggle with memorization. Often those who sight-read well have trouble memorizing and those who memorize quickly have trouble sight-reading. One basic rule: allow yourself a great deal of time. When you know you have a performance in eight weeks, start *now* to memorize. As with any skill, it can improve with practice and with varying the approach. Perhaps some of the ideas below may help you.

- Write out the words to the piece many times.
- Keep the words with you and memorize a line or two while driving, taking the subway, standing in line in the cafeteria, washing your clothes, and so on.
- Get a recording of *yourself* singing the piece and listen to it over and over and over. Make sure it is not a commercial recording or a recording of someone else. When we hear other people sing, we tend to pay less attention to the words and technique. We listen more carefully and critically to ourselves.
- Listen to your recording both with the score and without. Listen while resting or when first awake in the morning—it will likely go deeper into your unconscious mind.
- Find words that indicate the beginning or ending of different sections and then memorize the sequence of these cues.
- Spend time analyzing the relationship of text to vocal line and of vocal line to accompaniment. Do a harmonic analysis. Understanding how the music is constructed can help your mind to grasp it.
- Do a character analysis. Remembering the sweep of emotions and your motivation(s) can help in memorizing.
- Play the piece on the piano or any other instrument you play. Play it many times.
- Endeavor to hear the piece mentally and either conduct it or move in a free-form dance. This can help get the piece in your body.
- Visualize yourself performing the piece. Breathe deeply as if singing, and hear it in your head. This is a very effective way to check memory. Any places that you cannot remember are places you have not truly learned. In that case, it is time to relearn rhythms, notes, and words.
- Draw a picture of the unfolding of the story. Use symbols or stick figures and many colors. You might assign colors to the various emotions in the piece.
- Remember when you were a child and you learned something by heart? That means you cared about it; you loved it so that it became part of you. Be aware of bringing that kind of care, attention, and love to your practicing and you may find that memorizing becomes second nature.

4

HEALTH AND BODY AWARENESS

YOUR BODY *IS* YOUR INSTRUMENT

ONE CONCEPT THAT CAN TAKE SOME TIME for the singer to grasp is how physical singing can be. That is why it is important to practice or rehearse when you feel awake and full of energy. Then you are likely to use good support and body strength to undergird your tone, rather than allowing extraneous muscles in the throat and neck to become involved. A tried and true adage is that the singer should finish a lesson, rehearsal, or practice session with the throat feeling fresh but the body feeling tired from active support. In fact, one of the reasons for having at least a small amount to eat before singing is that with the proper amount of support and body energy, quite a few calories are burned. As a silly experiment, I once weighed myself before and after an hour's program of opera arias—I had lost five pounds!

If the idea of using your whole body when singing feels like an elusive concept, you might experiment with some of the following ideas:

First, do several stretches before you sing, not only head and shoulder rolls, but also diagonal stretches with your arms and windmills or the Yoga Triangle posture (Triconasana) to get a good stretch of the lower part of the body, including the legs (for more Yoga posture suggestions, please see chapter 2, "Practicing").

Sigh deeply while seated—feeling as if the sigh were coming from the bottom of your seat. Then stand and see if you can sigh on pitch (sol-do or 5-1) and keep that same feeling.

Imagine that your body is a hollow statue and fills up with air from your head to your toes when you breathe. Next sing a scale and imagine both the air and the tone going up the back of the body and over your head. This idea, loosely adapted from *The Tao of Voice* by Stephen Cheng (see Resources), has helped many people to feel more grounded, centered, and singing from their core.

When your teacher says that your breath management (support) is strong, try adding powerful emotions to the singing of scales and other warm-ups. Performing your vocalizes as if full of rage or intense mourning or infectious delight can help pull your entire body more fully into the singing process.

Take a particular song or aria that you are studying. Hearing it clearly in your head, dance to it in a free-form dance or conduct it. Then go back to singing and see if, when standing still, your body can continue to feel as involved.

Living in your body in general will help you to gain greater control of your body and use its energy when you sing. To this end, some bodywork would be helpful, more so than dance or sports, which focus on a product. Yoga, Tai Chi, Feldenkrais Method, and Alexander Technique are among the kinds of bodywork that help singers live in the moment and focus on the process.

You can absorb a great deal of kinesthetic body knowledge by watching experienced singers, especially opera singers. Go to live concerts, watch broadcast concerts and operas, or rent videos.

Because your body is your instrument, any kind of bodywork is extremely beneficial. Specifically, dance will help in energizing your singing and particular kinds of dances are actually used in various operas and shows. Bodywork of almost any kind, such as Yoga, Tai Chi, Alexander Technique, and Feldenkrais Method will help with energy in singing. They will also assist you in becoming more comfortable with your body, increasing your awareness of the flow of energy, and enabling you to more quickly detect misuse or strain while singing. Investigate colleges, your local YMCA, and area fitness centers for classes and lessons. As with finding good voice teachers or coaches, finding good bodywork instructors can often be most easily accomplished by asking around.

Exercise, Nutrition, and Rest

How many times have you heard it? We all need to exercise—whether it be aerobics classes, sports, swimming or dance classes—try to get a good workout a few times a week. Cardiovascular exercise is beneficial to overall health and to singing, because the heightened activity of the respiratory system helps it to stay healthy and to slough off phlegm. A good workout will also aid your body in resisting viruses and infections and it can elevate your mood. Since the vocal folds are in an extreme position (open) during exercise, it is wise to wait at least one hour before singing. Allow them to relax before making the kinds of technical demands and minute adjustments required in good singing. In all forms of exercise, keep breathing as you work out. Holding your breath puts a strain on the larynx.

Weight lifting and toning can be beneficial, with a few caveats. Toning the lower abdominal muscles will aid in your core body strength, in balance, and in supporting singing. Avoid stomach crunches, sit-ups, or other exercises aimed at firming the midsection. You need these muscles to be elastic and pliable in order to breathe well. A former student of mine decided to get himself a "six-pack" over the December/January semester break, only to find that he could not sustain tones or sing long lines until the *end* of the spring semester when the muscles finally relaxed! Be judicious with weight lifting. Unless you use primarily light weights for the arms, you are putting a strain on the larynx. It would be better to find other ways to work out.

In addition to exercise, singers need to eat healthy foods. A multivitamin can help, but researchers say the best way to get the vitamins we all need is from food—lots of fruits and vegetables. Singers also need to sleep as many hours as possible. Some find that not only does their tone quality differ when they have had less sleep, but even their range can shorten by a note or two. The mental sharpness from REM (rapid eye movement) sleep is essential for effective practice and performance, and scientists say that our best REM comes between the seventh and eighth hours of *continuous* sleep.

VOCAL HEALTH

The following information should never be considered a substitute for a doctor's advice. It is judicious for a singer to visit an otolaryngologist (ENT) when she or he is healthy, so that the doctor can look at the vocal folds and have a baseline for comparison when the singer is ill.

Old Man Winter

If you live in a northern climate, your task as a singer in winter is to stay hydrated, because the normal mucus present in your nose and throat tends to thicken from the season's dryness. The thicker the mucus, the harder it is for your body to slough it off and the more likely it is to become infected. Cold air itself is dry and is made worse by drying heating systems. Consequently drink as much water as you can stand—aim for two liters a day, double that if you are ill. The body recognizes sodas, juice, and coffee as food, not water; so make certain that your water intake is above and beyond your consumption of those beverages. If you drink alcoholic or caffeinated beverages, have some water along with them because they are very drying. Realize that your intake of water needs to be constant: how well lubricated your throat feels today is certainly affected by how much water you drank yesterday. Chugging some spring water before your lesson will not compensate for lack of hydration. In fact, some experts say that if you feel thirsty, you are already dehydrated. An adage many singers use is "pee pale, sing clear"—when you drink enough water that your urine is quite pale, you can be sure that your system is getting enough hydration to slough off phlegm and keep your instrument clear. (In this and all other vocal hygiene issues, do check with your doctor. Some bodies are more prone to losing vital electrolytes through overhydration, leading to serious health issues.) Buy a bottle of nasal saline spray and use it several times a day. Get some kind of steamer for your bedroom: cold-mist, vaporizer, or ultrasonic, depending on your budget. Often singers complain about the sensation of having too much mucus, but the sensation of too much phlegm is usually that it is too thick. The cure is hydration and the singer's best friend: Guaifenesin. It thins the phlegm and helps the body slough it off. You can take it in expectorant syrup or in pill form. Please ask your doctor about dosage.

Be winter wise: dress warmly, in layers. Going from the cold outside to overheated buildings is tough enough on your body; let it breathe by removing sweaters and other wraps. A scarf over your nose and mouth warms and moistens the air and a hat keeps your head from losing 90 percent of your body heat.

Winter is the time for colds and influenza just about everywhere; therefore wash your hands frequently with soap and water. The antibacterial waterless hand cleansers are convenient but do nothing against viruses.

Gum

There are two reasons to avoid gum chewing. First, it puts a great strain on the jaw and surrounding muscles because unlike food, what you chew is very small and does not break down. Any strain in the jaw and neck compromises your ability to have loose and free articulation and the strain radiates to the neck muscles, and ultimately, the larynx. Since singers are prone to gastro-esophageal-reflux disease (GERD, see below) it is wise to avoid chewing gum, because it promotes acid production by a stomach waiting for food. Even if you are not prone to GERD, it is still wise to avoid excess stomach acid.

Gastro-Esophageal-Reflux Disease

Gastro-Esophageal-Reflux-Disease (often called reflux) is extremely common among singers. A few years ago, an ENT in Boston interviewed voice majors from three music schools there and discovered that 80 percent had GERD. Scientists know that the active support used in good singing helps open the sphincter muscle, which allows the contents of the digesting stomach to travel up the esophagus and inflame the arytenoids (the cartilages that open and close the vocal folds). What scientists do not yet understand is why so many people with GERD have no burning sensation.

Symptoms of GERD can include heartburn, wheezing at night (the fumes from the digesting stomach create this), coughing at night (again from the fumes), difficulty singing or speaking in the morning, a sense of fullness in the throat, difficulty with high pitches, a feeling of sluggishness in the singing. You may have one or several of these symptoms. If you believe you do, it is imperative that you consult with an ENT. You can certainly try over-the-counter antacids and medications such as Prilosec, but these are no substitute for professional advice.

With an 80 percent chance of GERD, it might be wise to assume that you have it and to take precautions such as: exercise on an empty stomach (or just a small bit of mild food or milk); avoid eating for two hours before bedtime; minimize alcohol and caffeine consumption; be sparing with spicy food; avoid peppermint, soda, chocolate, and citrus; elevate the head of your bed; avoid smoke and gum-chewing; avoid garments that are tight around the middle; and try taking antacids before bed and one hour after meals. If it sounds like a lot, go with moderation. For example, have just one cup of coffee in the morning and if you have spicy food one day, avoid it the next.

If You Have Allergies

Avoid treating yourself for allergies with nonprescription drugs, because they usually have more ingredients than you need and can cause dehydration. Many students have complained to me over the years that their voice suddenly feels sluggish or unresponsive, not realizing that it was from medication, since their throats did not *feel* dry. Instead, find a good allergist or ENT and map out a plan for your health. If your doctor prescribes antihistamines, buy some Guaifenesin to thin your mucus and ask if you may have the least-drying antihistamine effective for your condition.

Buy yourself one of the personal steamers available in most drug stores for about $40. Breathing steam for five to fifteen minutes in the morning can make a world of difference in your health and in your singing.

Try irrigating your nose twice a day before using any prescription nasal sprays. Add half a teaspoon of salt to one cup of warm water. Lean over a sink and using a rubber ear syringe, squeeze the water into one nostril while holding the other closed. The water will come out of both nostrils and your mouth. Repeat and alternate nostrils until the water is used up.

If you have exercise-induced asthma, ask your doctor about using an inhaler before you practice. Some singers find that the physical activity involved in singing is enough to trigger their asthma.

If You Are Ill

When you are ill, cancel the audition or performance; postpone the rehearsal. You will damage both your voice and your reputation by trying to sing through illness. What you need to do is drink fluids and rest as much as possible. Avoid the temptation of "miracle" drugs—they are likely to contain drying agents that will simply mask symptoms and make singing more difficult and even dangerous.

Take some Guaifenesin and ask your doctor for a good cough syrup to soothe the reflex, as coughing is extremely hard on the vocal folds. Avoid throat clearing for the same reason. It can be annoying to feel the phlegm, but clearing just irritates the vocal folds and your body sends more phlegm there to protect them. Your job is to get well, and the best way is to rest.

Ease back into singing after an illness. If you have been coughing, it is smart to let the voice rest for three or four days after the coughing has stopped. Then you can start with some short periods of singing, gradually increasing as you continue to heal.

For Women

The hormonal changes in your menstrual cycle can have an effect on your singing. First, if you have premenstrual or onset bloat and swelling, your vocal folds will also have edema. Some women feel that the middle voice is sluggish, others have more difficulty with the top range, and others simply feel a veil over the tone. Take it easy vocally on those days because singing demanding repertoire on swollen folds can lead to hemorrhages or other problems. When you have control over the scheduling of performances, avoid setting performance dates during your period. It would be a good time to work on less demanding repertoire or use the time for analysis and memorization.

Medications

It is always a good idea to discuss both prescription and over-the-counter medications with your doctor. Sometimes, though, your primary care physician, and even your ENT, do not know what effects different medications can have on the voice. For that reason, when I visit my doctor, I take a printout from the National Center for Voice and Speech (http://www. ncvs.org). On their Web site, click "Information" and then "For Vocologists" to get a list of the two hundred most-prescribed medications and their effects on singing. Often there are two or three choices for any given condition. With my doctor's willingness and the list, we can choose one that will have the fewest effects on my singing.

The Fun Stuff

Okay, so high school and college years are a time for at least some fun. Just remember that as a singer, you need to have a healthy body to do your work. A good rule of thumb is: would an athlete in training do this? If not, then neither should you. Having said that, I know that partying and experimenting are part of the young adult experience. So, please use your head. When you plan to go to a rock concert and scream all night, be sure it is not the weekend before you perform in a seminar or master class. If you plan to indulge in substances, don't do it the night before a lesson or a performance.

HOW TO SURVIVE CHORAL REHEARSALS WITH YOUR VOICE INTACT

Choral singing can be exciting and rewarding and at the same time a source of vocal fatigue. Below are some suggestions for reducing the strain and increasing the pleasure.

- Always warm up before rehearsals. The best conductors use choral warm-ups, but you cannot count on that. You are in charge of your instrument so make certain it is prepared.
- Bring water and sugar-free lozenges to the rehearsal. Keep your throat moist and lubricated.
- Avoid talking during the rehearsal—both as a conscientious choir member who listens to directions and to lessen vocal fatigue.
- Sit tall—on the first third of the chair, with your feet flat on the floor. Poor posture encourages vocal strain.

- When possible, learn your part away from the rehearsal. Trying to focus on your own technique while learning notes, and surrounded by others who may not be singing correctly, is a recipe for strain.
- If you are ill, inform the conductor. Stay alert, breathe where you normally would, and follow along with the group. You can learn a great deal this way.
- Whenever you can, do some gentle stretches. If the conductor is working with another section for a few minutes, do some shoulder rolls or head rolls or massage your jaw hinge or lean forward and let your head drop between your knees. Muscular fatigue and tension can create vocal fatigue and tension.
- Avoid listening to yourself; aim to sing softly. When we try to hear ourselves, we usually push. If you are very concerned, cup an ear with one hand—that will usually give you some idea of how you sound.
- While it is important to blend and be part of the ensemble, it is also important to remain aware of your body. Find the tension and release it before it becomes discomfort or pain.
- If your ensemble's rehearsal is long, take some vocal breaks. Sing normally for twenty minutes, then for the next twenty minutes stay alert, breathe with the group, but just mouth the words.
- During the rehearsal break, be certain to get up and stretch and move around. Bring an apple or carrots or some other food that will make you chew quite a bit—the chewing is a good release for the larynx. If food is not allowed in the rehearsal space, you can release the larynx by gently chewing your tongue, as if you were chewing food. Be a sloppy eater in this—let your mouth hang open and your tongue protrude. Chew for about ninety seconds.
- Do not sing every repetition of difficult passages, but breathe and mouth the words. Take high notes down an octave if they are repeated many times.
- Suppressing vibrato is unhealthy. If your conductor insists on it for every piece, find another group to join! For an occasional piece, try singing softly and very hollow or hooty like a boy soprano. Find that laser beam of head voice and stay with it.

5

THE COMPLETE SINGER/MUSICIAN

MUSIC THEORY IS YOUR FRIEND

I KNOW OF A UNIVERSITY STUDENT who is constantly broke. Why? She refuses to take the time to learn piano or some other instrument, or solfege well enough to learn her music by herself. Consequently, she must pay a pianist to help her learn her music. Just a few months of intense piano study would solve that stumbling block, but she is "too busy"—and she's broke. It is a pity, because this student is not only spending money that could be used for other purposes, she is also gaining a reputation as a poor musician. Singers, beware! I was a pianist as an undergraduate, and I refused to accompany singers because they never knew their music. Instrumentalists, on the other hand, would show up to rehearsals knowing their music cold. Having been an instrumentalist as well as a singer, I am aware that instrumentalists expect singers to be poor musicians, especially regarding rhythm. On the other hand, when a singer comes into an orchestral rehearsal prepared and independent, the instrumentalists and the conductor (especially) take notice. Conductors obviously prefer to work with people who are prepared, as do coaches and accompanists. Making a good impression will aid your professional relationships and can lead to recommendations or even offers of work.

As mentioned earlier, some singers believe that the text will propel them and the accompaniment will carry them. Nothing could be further from the truth, especially in more advanced literature and in modern repertoire. Being a complete and independent musician should be every singer's goal.

I strongly recommend using piano or another instrument to learn to read music. It is very helpful to have a button to push or a key to press as you learn the lines and spaces, duration of notes, key signatures, and so forth. This kinesthetic learning of music is vital to becoming a confident musician. In singing technique, however, it is best if we do not feel things in the throat. Even solfege syllables can get one tied up in knots, especially if the range is very high or very low.

When possible, take some theory courses, especially those aimed at singers. Community colleges, college extension courses, and community music schools offer sight singing, ear training, and other music fundamentals courses. There is also a Web site that will help you learn the rudiments of music reading: http://datadragon.com/education/reading.

You may have heard stories that appear to be straight out of the movies: some singer learns a new opera role overnight to replace an ailing performer and becomes famous. It truly does happen. Being able to learn (and memorize) music quickly can lead to employment as a soloist, chorister, a "ringer," and more. When faced with two beautiful voices, if the conductor knows one is a better musician, that singer is hired.

IMMERSING YOURSELF IN SINGING

If you are studying voice with short-term goals in mind, you may want to skip this section. If, on the other hand, your lessons will be part of a longer-term avocation, or you are or plan to be a voice major in college, read on to see what other endeavors can help your vocal and musical growth.

There is much more involved in being a well-educated singer, performer, and musician than simply training muscles and learning the coordinations involved in good singing. Becoming a fine musician involves many subtle elements generally attained through listening and imitation. If, like me, you did not grow up absorbing the nuances of classical singing, it is vital that you immerse yourself in it now. As opposed to instrumental performance, vocal performance also requires facility in many ancillary areas, including languages, body awareness, and acting.

Ideally, classical singers should be exploring one new language for each year in college along with dance, bodywork, and acting. Do not put off these tangential but vital studies.

When I was a graduate student, I was frustrated at the number of traditions that were not written down anywhere. Appoggiaturas in Mozart recitatives, certain endings that are always taken in various songs or arias, portamenti in Italian literature, possible cuts in arias, and cadenzas in bel canto repertoire are only a few examples. Having come to singing later in life, I was often befuddled by these traditions that my colleagues (all voice majors as undergrads) seemed to know. As I soon discovered, even in this era of recordings, videos, and the Internet, classical singing is still an oral tradition. To become part of that tradition, it is vital to immerse yourself in the art. That means attending concerts whenever possible, asking questions of your teacher, coach, and colleagues, and listening, listening, listening. Accordingly I would put on vocal recordings during dinner or when entertaining and I would listen while doing homework, housework, or driving. I went to my local library and borrowed videos of operas and vocal recitals. I soon began to absorb many artistic aspects and translated them into my own singing, often without being aware that I was doing so.

Legato can be a particularly elusive quality to capture. Ask your teacher for examples of singers with good legato and listen with your eyes closed—seeing if your body can intuit what the singer does to spin that line. Also listen to string players as soloists or in ensembles. Perhaps hum or lip-trill along to get the feeling of constant motion—of the bow never leaving the strings.

Listen to all kinds of singers, not just those in your own range. Often sopranos will learn a great deal by listening to tenors negotiating high pitches. Ask your teacher for recommendations of different specialties: singers with wonderful spin and legato, singers whose diction is especially fine, or those with a warm tone. Find your own favorites and ask yourself why. Is it beautiful tone or intensity? Does the voice create a convincing character? Endeavor to nurture the qualities you most enjoy in your own singing.

Another way to immerse yourself in the world of singing is to read. There are many resources available on various aspects of singing, from books on technique and interpretation, to periodicals such as *Classical Singer* or *Opera News* that can inform you about the current vocal scene. How about setting a goal of reading one book every month on a vocal topic? Reading biographies of famous singers is a fun way to learn a great deal about the world of singing.

If you are studying voice in college or university, you are most likely required to study French, German, and Italian (and many now are adding Spanish to the list) along with lyric diction courses on those languages. If that is not your program's requirement, or you are not in school, aim to get some training in those languages. If you reside in or near a large city, there are language schools (such as the Goethe Institute for German) that offer reasonably priced language classes. Do not overlook community colleges, extension divisions of high schools or colleges, and your local YMCA. Maybe some summer courses or weekend immersion classes are possible.

As a last resort, there are very fine language training packages with tapes or CDs available at most bookstores. It is vital that you gain facility with each language so that, as with a native speaker, you will stress important words and bring an overall sense of meaning to everything you sing.

In college or university studies, avoid the temptation of taking easy courses to fulfill your liberal arts requirements. Your acting and your deeper understanding of both music and text will benefit from a solid grounding in history, literature, and poetry. When you are studying voice as an avocation, attempt to take such broadening classes at local community colleges or high school extension programs. You could also embark on a reading program to give yourself a solid grounding in Western civilization. Does this sound like a lot of work? Perhaps so, but if you read interviews with the best singers and actors, they all consider this an essential part of their preparation. The finest opera singers will research the era in which the opera is set, will read the original play or novel or story that the opera is based on, and will view videos or read books on the country in which the opera is set. The greatest actors do the same with the plays or movies in which they are cast. Remember that singing is not necessarily an end in itself—it is a form of expression—you need to bring something to it, you must have something to express. The most compelling singers are by and large those with rich, full, satisfying lives outside of music. Expand your horizons, expand your abilities, expand your experiences, and you will bring a wealth of life to express through your music.

Acting is of supreme importance. If you are in college or university and can take performance classes and acting-for-singers classes, also take some straight acting classes when possible. The conventions are different between spoken and sung productions, but the intense kind of inner exploration and character work normally involved in monologues and scenes will help all your performances. If you are not in school, again, check out local community colleges, university extension courses, high school extension courses, your local YMCA, and perhaps some music or dance studios.

6

A FEW WORDS ABOUT TECHNIQUE

IS THE TEACHER/STUDENT DYNAMIC WORKING?

THE INTENT OF THIS BOOK is to assist and complement voice lessons. Yet some discussion of technique cannot be avoided, especially when evaluating whether you are on the right track. So having found a voice teacher and started lessons and explored some of the other ancillary areas discussed thus far, let us evaluate the process.

1. First of all, are you in the driver's seat or do you present yourself passively for transformation? Students who take charge of their own development, who come into lessons with a plan (for example, "I need to check some technical aspects in song A and I need help with interpretation in song B"), are those who grow the fastest.

2. Do you record your lesson and listen to the recording at least twice—listening once with scores, taking notes, and once without the scores to absorb matters of artistry and interpretation? Do you also take notes, maximizing your retention of what your voice teacher is telling you?

3. Do you keep a practice log, noting date and time of practice, problems encountered, and remedies attempted, breakthroughs, and insights?

4. Do you practice regularly, ideally for one hour, five to six days a week?

5. Do you work on troublesome sections first or do you just run through your pieces?

alerting your teacher to difficulties, especially if, for ex-
ou leave practice times or lessons with tightness in the
a hoarse or scratchy voice? Teachers can tell a great deal
hey hear and see, but only you can play your instrument
and only you know whether it is truly comfortable. Be sure to speak
up! It is not a condemnation of his or her teaching, but a problem
for you both to solve.

Now on to some basic questions about your teacher:

1. Do you work well together?
2. Does the teacher welcome your ideas, questions, and insights or is
   he or she threatened, wanting a more dependent ("yes ma'am, yes
   sir") relationship?
3. Do you feel that technical matters are addressed on an individual
   basis, with the teacher trying several ideas to find one that works
   for you? Or is there a one-coat-fits-all mentality in the studio?
4. Does it seem as if the teacher listens to you, has time for you, and
   informs you of auditions, competitions, and performances? Or do
   you feel passed over?
5. Does the teacher help you stay in the moment with your singing,
   assisting you in the journey of becoming a singer or does she or he
   demand certain ends without respect for your individual process?
6. Does the teacher seem to have a sense of where you are now and
   where you might be headed? Does he or she have a vision for your
   future whether it is professional or amateur? Or do you feel that
   you and your vocal future are ignored?
7. Perhaps the two most important questions are: do you feel respected
   as a person in the studio and do you leave your lessons with a
   relaxed and free throat? If you ever feel badgered or belittled or
   you regularly leave lessons with a tight or painful throat, even after
   alerting your teacher *several times* of such discomfort, it is time for
   a change. Even if you live in a very remote area, there are always
   options for you. Maybe commuting twice a month to another area
   for lessons would be better than continuing with unsatisfying, even
   damaging, weekly lessons.

If you are attending a college, conservatory, or university program,
chances are you were assigned to a teacher. That does not mean that
you must stay with this teacher if you are not progressing or the studio
dynamic is uncomfortable. Unlike private lessons, you cannot simply
stop, but must go through some sort of procedure in order to change
teachers, and that is where your student handbook or departmental Web

site can come in handy. Some schools insist that all studio changes be made through the departmental chair or program coordinator. Others prefer that students speak with the current teacher and with a prospective teacher and work it out themselves. In any case, speaking candidly and diplomatically with your teacher can be the first step. It may be that you simply need to discuss progress, goals, and concerns. This may be enough to smooth out any difficulties and you both can go on in a more fruitful manner. On the other hand, a change may be in order. If, after trying your very best to work things out, it is still an uncomfortable situation, marshal all your forces to make a change. This is your major, your focus, and your future—do not settle for anything less than a cordial and productive working relationship.

SOME GENERALLY ACCEPTED TECHNICAL GOALS

While there are many theories and approaches when it comes to singing, there are some generally accepted goals. After a few years of study, one should be able to sing for a couple of hours without strain and tiring. As time and technique progress, so does the length of time that one can sing with ease. The tone should be free and unforced, and the scale even from top to bottom.

There was a time when voice teachers did not study anatomy in depth, or at all. Thus old school concepts of high breathing and pushing in with the abdominal muscles for support, for example, were developed. With so much research in the last few decades, that is no longer the case. Scientists now understand more precisely what happens in the body overall and the throat in particular, and as a result there truly is no excuse for poor instruction. If you are ever concerned or confused about the technical suggestions given you, please read any of the books by Richard Miller, Oren Brown, or others listed in the Resources section. In the two examples given above, we now know that low breathing will help to keep the larynx suspended, whereas high breathing can bring about tension. I am amazed to hear students who have been taught to "push in" for support. We now know that when one breathes, the sub-glottic pressure (the pressure of the air just below the vocal mechanism) is very strong and that pushing in to start the column of air flowing actually puts a strain on the larynx. On the contrary, one should resist in an energized way outward. Not pushing, but resisting the flow of air—as the Italians say, remaining appoggiato.

Legato is of ultimate importance in singing. You can think of it (as my teacher says) as "body-line"—the kind of body energy under the tone as if you were about to dance. Not only does energy make for legato, but also living in the vowel, not allowing upcoming consonants to color or shorten the vowel. This concept is diametrically opposed to the consonant-driven diction often espoused in choral singing. Naturally, it is important when twenty, thirty, or forty voices sing together, to stress beginning and ending consonants, but as a solo singer, you need to think and act in different ways. Your job is to make beautiful tone and only vowels can carry that for you. While forward, crisp consonants are important and can aid the listener in understanding the text, your chief focus needs to be on the vowel. Loose, forward, and relaxed articulation is the ideal. In attaining this ideal, a relaxed tongue and jaw are essential. If you have a lot of tongue and jaw tension, try doing some relaxation exercises before you sing.

In classical singing, it is also important to keep the vocal tract in an easy, fluid, passive position. You might think of it as keeping your mouth and throat in an open position no matter what the pitch and no matter what the vowel. There will, of course, be some slight shifts from vowel to vowel and note to note, but aiming for this openness will help with consistency of resonance and richness of tone.

PROBLEM SOLVING

As mentioned previously, one of the difficulties in teaching singing is that the instrument is hidden, out of view. I cannot play your instrument, nor can you play mine. Along with a hidden instrument is the elusiveness of some technical aspects. Some of the actions involved are involuntary or the coordinations are brought about by imagery or metaphor. One thing I have found helpful as a teacher is to know whether the student is primarily an auditory, visual, or kinesthetic learner. Then, if I am working on the concept of legato, for example, I might ask the auditory person to listen for the connection between notes—to avoid any space. I may ask the visual learner to imagine all the notes going away from them on a line over to the horizon and I could ask the kinesthetic person to feel as if they were singing in front of themselves. Some people are clearly and strongly one type of learner, others are strong in two areas, and still others are strong in all three. There are several resources for discovering which modality is your strongest. Two brief online tests are found at these sites:

> http://library.thinkquest.org/C005704/content_hwl_learningmodalities.php3
> http://712educators.about.com/cs/learnstyleassess/index.htm
> Balk, H. Wesley. *Performing Power*. Minneapolis: University of Minnesota Press, 1985, 66.

Once you have discovered your learning style, you can share that knowledge with your teacher. If it occasionally feels as if the two of you speak different languages, it could be that your modalities are different. Perhaps your instructor could rephrase directions and concepts in ways that make better sense to you.

One of the reasons for keeping a voice journal is to help in problem solving. Below are some of the most common problems I have encountered in my teaching and some solutions that have worked. Check with your teacher for further ideas and invent your own.

- Posture is a common problem because most of us slouch in daily life. One quick way to check if your body is in alignment is to simply rise up on your toes and then lower your heels. The other aspect of posture that feels foreign is how expanded the chest needs to be. I tell my students that there are aspects of singing that feel unnatural, but they are not unhealthy and a raised sternum with expanded chest is one of them. Women in particular, especially teenagers, feel self-conscious—as if they are displaying their bosoms for the entire world to see. A check in the mirror will show that this is not the case, but that one looks expanded and elegant. (Although I do joke with my female students, telling them to "Keep their high-beams on!") The singer can simply raise his or her arms over head, sense where the rib cage is, and attempt to keep it so expanded when the arms are lowered. Another method is to put a broomstick (or object of similar size) across the shoulders and under the armpits. Most singers find this to be very helpful—they breathe more deeply and support better as well.
- For support, I always ask a beginning student to blow up a big balloon, paying close attention to which muscles are involved. Those are the same muscles used in support. Some singers feel more effort around the solar plexus; others lower in the abdomen, others in the sides, and some in the back. Ideally, we should be gently resisting all the way around, as if trying to keep up an inner tube that is underinflated. Sometimes beginning students feel just a tightening or feel the muscles pushing inward. In that case, I ask them to redirect the muscles to gently resist outward. Then we go to exercises such as sliding on an "AH" from 1 to 5 and back to 1—seeing if they can use the same coordination, resisting long before they get to 5. Then doing the same slide but increasing it to 1-5-1-8 -1 without a break and, again, resisting long before reaching the 5 and the 8 (this exercise is example 4 in chapter 2, "Practicing").
- Another way to access support and especially helpful in singing high notes, is to think down. Gently resisting down and out is usually helpful, especially for those singers who tense when directed to use specific muscles for support.

- For ease in high notes or simply keeping passages brighter, it can help to feel as if you are singing through your eyes. Sopranos in particular are helped by imagining a direct connection from their support muscles to their eyes.
- Students who have trouble with rhythm benefit greatly from crawling! Eloise Ristad talks about it in her book *A Soprano on Her Head*:

> People with a strong sense of rhythm usually have a strong cross-crawl pattern. People with fuzzy rhythm, on the other hand, are apt to crawl by shifting weight from the right hand and right knee to the left hand and left knee.... You can change the "no sense of rhythm" curse if you can suffer the indignity of crawling around on all fours for a few minutes each day... concentrate on moving the left hand with the *right* knee and then the right hand with the *left* knee.... According to some specialists in developmental pediatrics, skipping the crawling stage can cause a gap in physiological and neural development. These gaps are also related to the sense of rhythm. (1982, 30)

> I can tell you that every student of mine who has tried the cross-crawling for a few minutes each day has improved dramatically in their rhythmic ability. Some have formed crawling teams in the dorms, going up and down the halls late at night!

- For drilling difficult sections of pieces, lip-trilling is excellent. It is highly unlikely to tense while trilling, so you can repeat difficult passages for quite a while without tiring the voice. (A secondary benefit is that lip-trilling can also help the singer to feel forward resonance and then track that resonance once they sing on words or a vowel.) For very tricky passages, especially fioratura work, I suggest lip-trilling backwards. This makes the mind focus and helps you to memorize the piece. In the example below,

lip-trill in a slow tempo, the E, D, and high C. Do this three times then add the G and F sharp and trill that combination three times, and keep adding pitches, working backward until you have the entire passage done and have lip-trilled it in its entirety three times. Then put the music away for a day. In a rather mysterious process, the unconscious mind continues to work on it and you will find the passage much easier next time you practice.

- For overall tension and especially fear of high notes, see if bending your knees in a balletlike deep plié as you go to the high pitch will help. Also try any of the following five movements while singing warm-ups (especially scales) and your repertoire:
- The weight of arms holds your head and you move your head side to side, keeping the chin parallel to the floor, looking far right then far left, independently of your body, slowly and gently.
- Cradle your head with one hand in the back and the thumb resting in the occipital joint (the indentation where the skull meets the spine and neck). Again, keeping your chin parallel to the floor, move your head from side to side, slowly and gently, but independently, without moving your body.
- Rest the little finger of one hand in the indentation just before the jaw hinge. The thumb rests gently on the throat and the rest of the hand on the back of the head and neck. Again, keeping your chin parallel to the floor, move your head side to side, independently of your body, slowly and gently.
- Cradle your jaw in your hand, as if stroking your beard and move your head side to side, keeping the chin parallel to the floor, as in the above postures.
- After you have tried some of the first postures, see if you can gently oscillate your head without any help from hands.

I first learned these movements in a workshop with Richard Miller and I have found them invaluable in my own singing and in teaching. Almost all of my students have enjoyed using these head movements, and their tone has immediately been richer and freer. It is no big secret that singers use movement. When you watch videos of Pavarotti singing, he moves his head ever so slightly before high pitches, to help the tone be free. We do tend to forget that in our fast-paced lives, we carry a great deal of head, jaw, and neck tension from driving, carrying books and bags, computer work, emotional tension, and so forth. Using some gentle movement in singing can help release the tone along with these daily tensions.

- For accessing the head voice, women benefit from making siren sounds or little child whiney sounds, and then carrying that down via octave slides or 5 tone descending scales into the middle and chest registers. On their own, the muscles figure out the register changes and the singer can focus on other matters. For men, it helps to do octave slides down from the falsetto into the upper and middle ranges keeping those lower pitches lighter and feeling like falsetto. Again, the body takes over negotiating the ranges.

- For overall energy, support, vibrancy of tone, and living in the vowel, I ask students to sing like an opera singer—a caricature of one, a nightmare of one, with whatever music we are working on. This has never failed to bring about an instant transformation. And contrary to the student's fears, they do not sound like an opera singer. Instead, their sound is richer, fuller, well-supported, and released, yet still their sound.
- When it feels as if your airflow is stuck or there is a lack of motion in your sound or you feel you might be squeezing the sound, try rotating your arms around each other at waist height. That usually helps the body to release the air and spin the tone. Another aid is to get a Slinky toy and move it constantly from hand to hand—attempting to match the movement with your airflow and tone. Tossing a tennis ball back and forth between your hands can also work.
- The way we use our voices in speech carries over into how we sing, and many of the voices we hear on the airwaves are very poor models. Most Americans speak too low in pitch and too far back in the mouth and throat, without support and resonance and without much variation in tone. One way to get yourself in a better groove is to warm up your speaking voice early in the day. Then when you go to sing, your voice will not be tired from misuse and will likely warm up for singing more quickly. My favorite way to do this is to count in a singsong way with lots of throat and mouth space, as if trying to sound like Julia Child. I count from one to thirty in groups of five, breathing at the end of each group. I elongate the speech, in the most singsong way, and vary the pitch widely.
- To avoid gasping while breathing and using throat muscles while singing, simply expand the body to breathe or think "yawn" rather than "breathe." Then when you go to sing, do not change anything in your throat. This takes some patience and some practice. Keeping your sternum raised and your ribs expanded is essential here. It is also helpful to consciously tell your throat to release and expand between repetitions of exercises or phrases of music. The larynx often wants to rise as we rise in pitch or as we expend our air. We need to teach ourselves to release and keep that relaxation.
- For ease in singing high pitches, find ways to relax, have fun, and be experimental. Actually move your head or body while singing. Try just touching the pitch and then descending, gradually increasing the time on the note. Try the note and the phrase it is in down an octave, sense what that feels like, and then see if you can sing it where it belongs with that much ease in the throat and simply more support. Go back and forth several times. Then put it away. Take

several days to try different approaches, perhaps use the passage as part of your warm-up.

- If you have an especially long aria or song, it can be helpful to practice the last few pages first. We often start strongly and then stop to work on sections, then start again, so that the first few pages are well learned and "in" the singer's body. We need to feel confident and at ease at the end of the piece as well. Practicing the last few pages alone will build muscle memories of singing it when you are fresh and energetic.
- Generally we want the body to be relaxed and the muscles in the throat and neck to be passive. Yet there are, to my mind, three areas that need some effort: be aggressive about support (resistance); be aggressive about body expansion, including keeping the sternum raised; and be aggressive about raising the soft palate—especially for higher pitches. Many singers feel a properly raised soft palate to be not only up, but forward, as if being pulled into the nasal cavity. When you sense the need to create more space, make it with a raised palate rather than overdropping the jaw (which can actually close the throat to some degree). You may well find that if you focus energy and effort in these three areas, that many other problems will simply disappear.

7

PERFORMING

WORKING WITH AN ACCOMPANIST

AN ACCOMPANIST CAN MAKE OR BREAK YOU in audition and performance situations and good accompanists and coaches can further your vocal, musical, and dramatic growth in profound ways. Therefore, it is vital that you take measures to nurture this relationship.

First, always give your accompanist good scores. Originals are best and often required for auditions and competitions. Be sure when you photocopy the score that you do not cut off part of the accompaniment. For your audition package it is customary to make front-to-back copies in a black binder. Some people use tabs to help in locating the song or aria or a list at the beginning of the music. In no case should you use plastic covers or staples: think of glare and injured fingers! Even the matte plastic covers can create glare in certain kinds of light. Cleanly indicate in bold black marker any cuts, or important changes in tempo or dynamics. When there are several cuts or other changes from the score, it is wise to take a moment in an audition to speak with the accompanist.

In auditions, if the accompanist starts your piece too slowly or too quickly, simply ask the adjudicators to start again. Turn to the accompanist and give him or her your tempo by quietly singing a few bars. In fact, it is generally a good idea to give your tempo through singing because it will more accurately reflect your performance. When we conduct or count out the tempo, we rarely keep in mind tempo variations and our overall speed may be faster than we can actually sing. Never snap your fingers (it is rude) or in any way blame the accompanist. Very often that person is the music director of the company! Always thank the accompanist when your audition is finished.

If you can find an accompanist with whom you like to work and can build a relationship, that is fortunate indeed. Whenever possible, use your regular accompanist for auditions—you have worked together, you have felt the ebb and flow in the music together—this will give you an edge. Always treat your accompanist like the gold mine that person is: be respectful of time and deadlines, pay on time or in advance, and give him or her difficult music in advance of a rehearsal.

When there are problems in rehearsal, be aware of how you phrase concerns. The best professionals take on the blame, such as, "We didn't seem to be together in those last two phrases. Did I count it wrong?" Being open to correction and flexible is not the same thing, however, as being compliant. Some singers act as if ensemble work involves just repeating what they did alone while others are so eager to measure up that they abandon themselves and their ideas in the pursuit of gaining acceptance. Neither approach is fruitful. An ensemble is best made up of strong individuals who will give and take. If you have a powerful feeling about the interpretation of a piece, talk about it. Be ready to do some compromising, but if it comes down to a match of wills, perhaps it is time for a different accompanist.

WORKING WITH A VOCAL COACH

Vocal coaches are underpaid geniuses. In comparison with instrumental music, vocal music has so many more unwritten traditions and variations from the printed page. A coach can help you understand these traditions and what conductors may be looking for in a particular piece. She or he is often expert at languages, interpretation, and helping the singer understand the larger sweep of a piece. Try coaching with people who have different specialties. You will find some who specialize in oratorio, others in opera only, some who specialize in cabaret music or musical theatre, and some who enjoy recital work. Working with a coach who is also a conductor helps in many ways. That person is out there in the field, knows what orchestras, choruses, or stage companies are looking for, and is usually abreast of auditions and other developments. Often when such a coach/conductor sees that a singer is open to direction, works hard, is a good musician, continues to grow, and acts in a professional manner, they hire that singer.

Be aware that coaches listen for a final product. You need to interpret their requests to match your technical understanding and present level of development. For example, a piece may call for a pianissimo high C. You may not be able to do that at this point in your progress, and you need to be able to articulate that to the coach. Perhaps saying, "That's a lovely idea and I will work on it with my teacher" will suffice. In the same vein, a coach should never take on the role of a teacher. Asking for particular elements of interpretation, for diction, for dynamics, or other effects are all within the coach's realm. Telling you how to do those things is not.

Finding a good coach is similar to finding a good teacher. Ask around. Go to concerts and take note of those accompanists who support the voice and move with the singer. Working with a coach who loves the voice is exciting. A true intimacy develops with give and take between performers. Subtle shifts occur in your concept of the music and the performances are full of life. Settle for nothing less!

ACTING AND STAGECRAFT TIPS FOR SINGERS

As mentioned in the section on analyzing your music, it is vital that you understand word-for-word what you are singing about. The overall presentation and word emphases are believable when you truly live with the text and make it your own. By the same token, becoming so familiar with the role that the character comes alive brings excitement and believability to your performance.

Characterization

When you do your character analysis, find ways in which the character is like you. For those aspects that are unfamiliar, search for even the smallest kernel of that within yourself. For example, I am not much of a flirt and never have been. Yet when faced with presenting flirtatious characters, I had to delve deeply within myself. Upon reflection, I realized that I *had* been a bit of a show-off and flirt as a little girl, but that behavior was socialized out of me. By getting in touch with that little girl who loved to be the center of attention and slightly outrageous, I was able to bring some life to flirtatious opera characters.

When you are in an opera or a show or you are singing several songs or arias by a particular character, make a point of living inside that character's head for a week or so. Do the dishes as she or he would, walk down the street as she or he would, take a bath as the character would. Keep a journal of all the ideas and insights that come to you and then take a fresh look at the score, seeing if there are new understandings of the music and possibly new places for movement or gestures.

Mechanics

When you walk on stage, whether in an audition, jury, or performance, walk slowly and lead with your sternum (your breastbone) in an expanded, proud posture. Smile at your audience and take the stage; it is now your turn so be big and alive and confident—whether you feel that way or not. First impressions are lasting and usually made within the first thirty seconds of a performance. Playing the part of a very confident, seasoned performer will do much to give a good impression and, eventually, will help any nervousness to recede. It may feel odd and it may seem as if everyone will know that you are just playing the part of the diva or divo, but actually no one will know and it will simply make you look confident.

If it is a performance, when you reach center stage or the crook of the piano, take a bow along with your accompanist (if it is a jury or audition, do not bow) and then take a moment of preparation. It is the singer's version of drawing the curtain—allowing you to get in character. It also allows the audience to clear their minds of what went before, not unlike a cleansing bit of sherbet in between courses of a rich meal. The convention is to look down at your feet, which closes you off from the audience for a moment. Then you can take a few deep breaths and think about the most important technical aspect and the most important interpretive aspect of the song. When you raise your head, the accompanist knows to begin. Be sure to raise your head slowly and in character. Then find a focus slightly above the heads of the audience. Your song may have one focus or several. If you sing about how much you love spring, you may look at a center focus and see the trees and the birds and their nests and so forth. The audience cannot tell what you are seeing; it simply makes you look engaged. Be aware that you need to start this focus and engagement from the moment you look up and maintain it during introductions, interludes, and postludes. In fact, interludes can be ideal times to shift focus and mood. When you sing about spring and its wonders and that reminds you of your lover and the wonders of him or her—then you need two foci—one for spring and one for your lover. Perhaps you could start center with spring and then move your eyes slowly to one side for the lover. Do not go too far left or right with your focus, as that would make it difficult for the audience to "read." When you change focus, unless it is a very dramatic moment with a quick shift, change the focus slowly in time with the music and keeping your eyes just above the audience. Do not look down to change focus unless it is a moment of great pain for your character, otherwise it looks weak or hard to read.

If you have a set of songs, it can be more interesting for the audience if you choose different foci. I prefer to put objects of interest to one side or the other and use center focus for expressions of pure emotion. Once you have done a fair amount of performing, and you have a song that is telling a story or a joke directly to the audience, you can experiment with looking at the audience and at a focus. I do not recommend this for beginners, because looking directly at the audience can disrupt your concentration or make you feel nervous.

Often various foci and a quiet body with an expressive face are all that is needed for a moving performance. Sometimes you may want to take a different stance—perhaps lean against the piano a bit for a more relaxed or sultry look or put one arm up on the lid while standing in the crook for a formal kind of look, or step forward with your arms behind you to indicate intensity or sincerity. There are many kinds of stances and moods, which is why it is important to practice them and discover the best fit for you. Do you know a coach who can help with staging? Then certainly ask for such assistance. Otherwise, use a mirror or get a friend to videotape a rehearsal for you. Seeing your performing with your own eyes is invaluable—you can see what does or does not work and come up with new ideas.

When you choose to gesture, practice with the music (even if just in your head) and with a mirror. Gestures need to be in time with the music. For art songs and musical theatre songs, they usually can be moderately sized. For opera arias, they need to be larger. Save the biggest gestures for the highest points of drama, or the end of the piece. For general believability, asymmetrical gestures are best. Be careful not to cover your face. If you choose to take a step for dramatic purposes, time it with the music as well, generally stepping just before you sing an important phrase or note. Never cross one leg in front of the other and never step backwards—both look insincere or confused or weak. When there is a dramatic moment of fear or surrender, you might take a step backward, but generally, using facial expressions or gestures would work better. Again, as with stances and foci, getting a video of yourself taking steps or gesturing would be of infinite value.

In the midst of singing and changing focus and using gestures and everything else, keep a part of your mind on your technique and especially on your breathing. One of our tasks as performers is to put the audience at ease. When the audience sees you walk out confidently (whether you feel that way or not) and take the time to breathe, they relax, and are all the more receptive to your performance. This is another aspect in which solo singing is different from choral. In choral singing we are often admonished to take a breath quickly and get back in, frequently we can "stagger breaths" with our section partners. For solo singing, this quick breathing can lead to tension and to having inadequate breath for the phrase. As a soloist, it would be helpful to think of your breathing as part of the singing or as an important prelude to it, not something to be done quickly and gotten over. My favorite analogy is watching a baseball pitcher. To my mind, half of the satisfaction in a good pitch is the wind-up. In singing, look on your breathing as the wind-up. You can also set the mood by how you breathe, and by considering it part of your expression. If the next line you sing is full of joy, take the breath in a joyful way.

When we make mistakes in performance, it is too tempting to "telegraph" that to the audience. By a grimace or a shrug we let them know that we are not oblivious or ignorant, but quite aware that we have erred. It can be a strange way of apologizing for the mistake. Please do not give in to such temptation. It is both inelegant and unprofessional. Many errors are never detected by the audience and for those incidents where the mistake is glaringly obvious, your listeners will be much more impressed by your composure and poise in ignoring the mistake and staying focused on the music, the story, and the character. Practice this kind of composure, remaining in character, and staying with the line of the story and song in your rehearsals and practice sessions. Especially when you are getting close to a performance date, do not stop for mistakes or indicate errors. Keep the kind of poise you desire for your performance during practice, and it will soon become habit.

No matter how well you believe your performance went, always bow and smile. Even if it was not your best, you have given the audience the gift of your performance and they want to acknowledge that gift with their applause. Refusing to bow *never* looks as if the performer were shy or humble or upset with themselves; it always looks rude—as though the performer were refusing the audience's return gift of applause. Therefore save your complaints and self-chastising for later. Take a deep bow, leading with your head, with open arms (avoid crotch-covering hands), and come up with a smile. Then either turn to the pianist with your back to the audience—which gives the pianist the stage—or make a slow, sweeping gesture to the pianist. If the audience continues to applaud, bow again briefly, and leave the stage. The singer always leads in both entering and exiting.

PERFORMING

Below are some hints for performance preparation from the point of view of preparing for a recital. They should be tailored to your needs—a one-song performance does not require this much preparation while an operatic or musical theatre role may require more.

Performance Preparation

Make certain that your music is memorized at least a month in advance. You then have time for the music and words to settle and to work on acting and interpretive factors. Memorizing at the last minute is courting disaster.

Record your practice sessions and listen with a critical ear. This is especially important for your sessions with your accompanist. Listen once with the music, noting any changes or suggestions you have for yourself. Listen once without the music, as objectively as you can, to see if it is a moving or compelling performance.

Practice performing, not just singing:

1. Use a mirror to check facial expressions and gestures—you can even lip-sync to a recording of your latest rehearsal, focusing on your stagecraft.
2. Sing through your program, taking breaks no longer than you will in performance.
3. Work as often as you can with your accompanist.
4. Ask trusted friends to watch rehearsals and give you feedback.
5. When possible, have some rehearsals videotaped. It is invaluable for you to see your own performing.

Mental Preparation

Analyze your music. When you take the time to know your scores intimately, seeing the interplay between voice and accompaniment, and understanding the text word-for-word, you may feel as if you wrote the piece. In many subtle and powerful ways, your performance of the piece will be enhanced.

- Study your scores frequently. Imagine yourself performing the pieces, remembering what the different passages felt like when last you sang them, and even breathing at the appropriate places. This silent work will do a lot to ensure a solid performance—it is similar to the visualization that competitive athletes use. Create an actual sense of how you want to feel in your body. Using images and sensations rather than words activates the right hemisphere of the brain, which can help create a feeling of calm, and "program" yourself for calmness in performance.
- When the performance date is just a few weeks away, develop a list of important points you want to remember for each piece. By a few days before the performance, trim your list to the most important technical point for each song and the most important interpretive

point. You can even memorize this list. Then, when you are taking your moment of preparation before the song, you can be thinking, for example, "Everything above the hard palate, keep a sense of yearning." As with the visualizing, if you can come up with images and sensations for each piece, your body will better remember and utilize them in performance.

- Singers often experience a sense of being stale at some point between first learning the music and the final performance. This might be the time to take out the list from chapter 1, "Getting Started" and find the list of steps for learning a song. Once the fundamentals of learning a piece and getting it "in" your technique are in place, using some of the "zany" ideas listed there can be helpful in owning the piece. They can also help to revitalize it when it feels stale. In her recording *The Creative Fire*, the noted Jungian psychoanalyst, author, and lecturer Dr. Clarissa Pinkola Estés discusses the creative process in detail. She urges the listener to allow a playful approach to lead the way because play uses the deeper self and allows for discovery of new things. When you feel stale, that is precisely what you need to do: find some new elements in the piece or new colors in your voice or new subtleties in your interpretation. Singing it in an opposite mood, mocking the song, singing it as if you were someone else, using props or huge crazy gestures—the list can go on and on. Give yourself a session or two or more to just have fun. If you have an accompanist who is open to this process, the two of you can have a wonderful time truly playing together and it will give the actual performance of the music much life and sparkle.

A large part of the singing process involves using the left hemisphere of the brain—the analytical, rational part. It is important and necessary to do this. Yet the most expressive singers also make great use of the right brain—the intuitive, nondirectional part. Another tool that the creative self uses is deep observation. When you are feeling stale or stuck it might be time to go to a concert or find a video of a well-seasoned performer singing the music you will be performing. Just observing and letting the music and the acting wash over you will help stir your own creative juices.

Physical and Psychological Preparation

For several of the suggestions here, I am indebted to Don Greene's book *Performance Success* (see Performance Anxiety: An Annotated Bibliography).

- Look on your performance as a marathon and prepare as an athlete does for such an event. Eat nourishing food, drink lots of water, and get as much sleep as possible.
- You might be too excited to sleep much the night before, so be sure to get extra sleep the previous week. It is a good idea to carbo-load two days before (you will be using this energy in performance) and sleep at least ten hours that night.
- It is best to schedule your dress rehearsal at least four days before the concert. That way, you can have time to listen to the recording and absorb what you learned in that performance. Such scheduling also allows for several days of vocal quiet (singing minimally and studying your scores). At that rehearsal, wear your performance outfit. Then you can be sure that nothing hinders your breathing and supporting. Especially note if your shoes help you feel grounded. If not, get a different pair!
- When your performance is an entire program, or even half a program, be kind to yourself as the date nears. It would be helpful, about three days prior, if you could postpone meetings and put off projects. Use your time to visualize your performance, to do relaxation exercises, and pamper yourself. Spend more time in mental rehearsals and less in physical and technical ones.
- Realize that as you get closer to the performance date, you will have some fears and doubts. When you experience a moment of anxiety, just remind yourself that it is normal and go on with your day. Write your fears in your journal, take time to pray or meditate, use nervous energy to exercise or go for long walks.
- In the forty-eight hours before a performance, be especially good to yourself. Take walks, read good books, watch funny movies. Plan ahead and schedule a massage for the day before. It is vitally important to safeguard your energy. Stay off the telephone and talk as little as possible. (When we talk on the phone, we often use higher frequencies and a louder tone in general, leading to vocal strain.)
- On the day of the performance, it is normal to have a major drop in energy. Do not try to compensate by consuming caffeine, sugar, and starch. Your body is pulling together its resources for the performance. Take a nap or a hot bath if that will make you feel rested and refreshed but be alert and awake by four hours prior to the performance. Also be sure that any meal is eaten at least four hours before the performance. Make it a medium size meal of nutritious, easily digested food. Warm up slowly and carefully—just twenty minutes at a time with breaks. Fruit for energy can be eaten

right up to the time when you walk on stage. Stay away from dairy, chocolate, and any other food that creates phlegm.

- When the audience greets you with applause as you walk on stage, breathe it in, and imagine yourself embracing them. Take a lot of time to breathe deeply and prepare: everyone, including the audience, needs a transition into the concert. As you prepare, hear your piece as you would like it to sound, then breathe deeply, and sing from your heart. Enjoy!

8

A BRIEF LOOK AT PERFORMANCE ANXIETY

THE MOST IMPORTANT THING TO KNOW ABOUT STAGE FRIGHT, the point with which I start all my workshops on overcoming performance anxiety, is that you are not alone. All of us have bouts of nerves, depending on the stakes involved. You may look around at your colleagues and wonder why no one else suffers. The truth is that most people have performance anxiety from time to time, many never admit to it, and many cope by throwing diva-fits or trying to undermine their colleagues or turning to vices. What is crucial is how you handle the butterflies.

If you view having performance anxiety as a flaw of character, as something only you experience, as a deep dark secret, then chances are you avoid dealing with it. You push it down and attempt to cope by avoidance. Then when the butterflies inevitably emerge, your view of yourself as impaired, as the only one who is struggling, as a less capable person and singer is reinforced, and after you are finished feeling bad about yourself, you may wonder why you put yourself through such misery.

Take heart and take charge! Start today on a journey to learn why the anxiety exists, to work through the conflicts and emotions involved, and eventually to overcome the crippling effects of stage fright. At the end of this book is an annotated bibliography of what I believe are the best books available on performance anxiety. Most of them are readily accessible at your local library, bookstore, or through online booksellers. Because there are numerous books, workshops, and seminars available, I will just outline here some strategies for avoiding crippling stage fright and turning the butterflies into excitement. These strategies include performance preparation, mental preparation, and some backstage tricks.

PERFORMANCE PREPARATION

First, be sure to have ample, varied practice. No amount of creative visualization or relaxation exercises can make up for inadequate musical preparation. Avoid just going through the motions as you practice. Find ways to spice up that time, from having it videotaped to watching yourself in a mirror to asking trusted friends to watch and give feedback. Occasionally, mime along with a recording of your singing in front of a mirror or video camera to see if your presentation is polished and your acting believable.

When you feel that your performing is getting stale, try a few zany sessions. Sing everything as strictly as possible and then as over-the-top, hammy, melodramatic as you can, or try performing each piece with huge operatic gestures and stances. Another time, sing everything in its mirror opposite: with a tragic, mourning piece, sing it full of infectious laughter and joy. Approach a light-hearted song or aria, as if you were conveying the most tragic news in the world. After trying these experimental methods, sing the piece normally and notice if there is a transfer of energy—if some new life has been breathed into your performance.

As you practice, find ways to engage your right brain (pictures, sensations) in your singing. Imagine that you breathe through the soles of your feet or your whole body sings. Or imagine that your body is about to take off in flight or in an energetic dance and, instead, you channel that energy into the singing. We want to engage the right brain because it can lead to greater relaxation and help us stay in our bodies during performance.

Spend equal amounts of time studying your scores as you do practicing them. It is vital to hear the music in real time—do not rush through. Breathe where you would breathe in performance and hear the piece as you would like it to sound. This is similar to the kind of visualizing that Olympic athletes do—a skier may visualize the slope and sense where her body would need to lean and turn and so forth. As Eloise Ristad says, it's "muscle memory in reverse" (see Performance Anxiety: An Annotated Bibliography). Here is where we can make the two hemispheres work together. Using the right brain to hear the piece as you would like it to sound and to sense what would go on in your body, you can also be making notes about technical aspects or reviewing things you have written in the score—allowing the analytical left brain to work in conjunction with the right. This kind of analyzing and visualizing your scores will give you great rewards when you sing. You can then leave the analysis behind and your practice can be more sensory and right-brained, which will allow for greater relaxation and grounding in performance.

As mentioned in the previous chapter, it is vital to practice performing, including how you walk on stage, bow, and so forth. You want to guarantee success by practicing every aspect of the performance so that nothing can surprise you or take you off guard. A story is appropriate here. Some years ago I was singing in the choir at the Cathedral of Saint John the Divine in New York City. We were about to process and sing an Evensong service for which we had rehearsed the music, but never practiced the processing or any other details. For her own enjoyment, the actress Linda Lavin was singing with us for a while and I was her processing partner in this service. Now this was a woman who had a major television series in the 1970s and who had many theatrical credits, including having just won a Tony award for her stage performance in *Broadway Bound*. She touched my arm with an ice-cold hand and said, "I'm so scared, I'm about to throw up." Why? Because despite all her experience, she was out of her comfort zone. We had not gone through the mechanics of the service and it was, therefore, scary to her.

Another way to think of preparing for success and comfort is to consider how loving parents help a small child with a move. They take the child to the new home, walk through it, play some games in it, and maybe explore the neighborhood. That makes the new and potentially scary into the familiar. When we perform, we need to make our vulnerable inner selves comfortable by leaving nothing to chance and making the process familiar and comfortable.

MENTAL PREPARATION

Give equal weight to mental and psychological preparation as you do to musical preparation. Take that scared part of you by the hand and assure her or him that you will be there and you will help. Then do it! Learn some relaxation exercises from the books available or take a Yoga or Tai Chi class and practice these exercises daily. That way, the exercises are ready and available, like tools in a toolkit, to fight the clammy hands and shaky knees. For example, I regularly practice some Yoga asanas (postures) and take classes as often as I can. Then, when I am backstage and doing a few asanas to expand my posture and relax, I feel not only the benefits of those postures but also the positive, relaxed memories of class. Just remembering the class helps transfer some of that calm and centeredness to the present time and it stays with me in performance.

Practice visualizing your performance. In real time, see yourself walk on stage, bow, prepare, and sing. Hear yourself sing beautifully, see yourself looking vibrant and confident. It works best if it is repeated many times before a performance, starting several weeks prior. You might try some affirmations, which also work best if repeated many times. The unconscious mind cannot discern positive from negative, so if your affirmation says "I will not be nervous" the unconscious will hear the "nervous" without the "not." It is better to say something in the affirmative, such as, "Whenever I perform I feel confident and centered." Write your affirmation as an already accomplished fact, not something in the future, which is also confusing to the unconscious mind. Post your affirmations around the house, say them aloud while driving, keep them on an index card and say them mentally while waiting in line. You may find a tremendous benefit from this kind of mental rewiring.

Another aid to relaxation is focus. This is normally developed over time, which is why it is helpful to perform as often as possible. A few years ago, the wonderful mezzo-soprano Frederica von Stade was interviewed by *Classical Singer* magazine. She discussed performing and stage fright, saying that so much of the work of performing has already been done for us by wonderful composers and librettists, if we attend to the text—to what we're singing about. Thinking, "Oh, I have to impress the director so she rehires me," or "I want to show my former teacher that I can really sing well," or "There might be someone in the audience who will hire me for future gigs," or "I'm so nervous that so and so is here," and similar thoughts, are all distractions and externals, according to von Stade. Our job is to tell stories and move audiences. Period. Coming to accept and embrace that "job" can take a lot of the pressure off. Learning that kind of focus, being able to dismiss the distractions and externals, and attend to the task at hand, can come through performance classes, workshops, and simply performing as often as you can.

Another mental strategy is to make a checklist ahead of time. Don't get too complicated, just set a few goals. Possibly in this performance you want to focus on keeping your breathing calm and your acting animated but not interfering with technique. Afterward, give yourself a percentage of how you did in performance as compared with rehearsals. The soprano Elisabeth Schwartzkopf used to say that if we can do 75 percent as well in performance as we do in rehearsal, that is good. And she was an international opera star! Keeping goals and lists and percentages can also lend a feeling of experimentation, of a laboratory-style approach, so that no one performance has so much weight to it. That can also take the pressure off.

BACKSTAGE TRICKS

- Play the part of the diva/divo. Contrary to most singers' fears, no one will know that you are doing this; you will simply look poised and confident. When you are especially afraid, pretending that you are confident can break the fear cycle.

- If you have a picture of yourself at age four or five looking happy and confident, with a big grin, take that picture backstage with you. Keep reminding yourself that the same child who knew no fear, who was ready to "go out there and shine" is still inside of you and still ready to be the one in charge—not that critic who also lives inside your head. Smile at the picture, breathe the essence of your kid self in, and then go out and enjoy!
- Some folks find it helpful to get to a window and gaze out. Seeing the train go by that will go by again at the same time tomorrow, helps lessen the weight of what they are about to do. Life will go on.
- Generally, it is a good idea to be alone backstage, even if the only option is facing a corner. Nervous chatter pulls anyone off center and scatters his or her energy. Breathe in deeply through your nose (to humidify the air) and focus on hearing at least the beginnings of your pieces, as you would like them to sound. Keep the breathing going! It is usually the first thing to go when nerves strike; so conscious attention to it while backstage will help keep the deep, calm breathing going when you are onstage. If you find it hard to get your breath low in your body, try putting the tip of your tongue on your hard palate, just in front of the uvula. Most people find their breathing soon becomes lower and calmer.
- Some singers like to keep a notebook or journal of all the positive comments, critiques, reviews they have received. This can include notes, articles, cards, and just jotting down words of praise. Reading this backstage just before performing can get the singer pumped up and prepared for success.
- If you have been working with some affirmations, select one that is working well for you or seems the strongest. Breathing deeply and walking slowly, say the affirmation over and over in your head while you wait for your turn onstage.
- Trying to block out the audience almost always fails, because they make you aware of their presence very easily. Therefore, when you walk onstage and during your performance, imagine that you breathe the audience in and cover them with your sound. This connects you to them in a positive way while putting you in a position of power.
- When you are feeling especially frightened, cold, stiff, pulled in, try getting angry. Think of all the crummy words folks have said or all the auditions that didn't go your way or the opportunities that you didn't receive. Go from small and powerless to expanding and angry and powerful. Then allow that anger to turn into pure power and even compassion and embrace the audience with it. This

transformation can take some time, so start this meditation at least a half-hour before you go onstage.

- Do some stretches, some Yoga asanas (postures), and even some calisthenics. Keeping your body moving and breathing deeply helps with energy and with staying focused and in your body when you perform. Do some shoulder rolls, some easy and careful head and neck rolls. Hang from your waist in a rag-doll fashion, looking down at your toes with your knees slightly bent. Let your head be heavy and your neck relaxed. Breathe deeply into the small of your back. Roll up slowly from the base of your spine, so that your head is the last to come up. Then rise up on your toes, arms stretched above your head. Lower yourself down onto your heels, and keeping your ribs in the elevated position, lower your arms. That series of movements should have expanded your body and prepared you to sing.

- Many performers find it helpful to take some humorous books or magazines backstage. Getting our funny bones tickled can help us put things into perspective and can bring energy and expansion to our performing.

- While onstage, some singers like to imagine that they are not alone. Having their imaginary back up singers can help them feel supported and relaxed. Again, this is something to practice in rehearsal so that your imagination and visualization are ready tools to help in performance.

- The last backstage trick involves a longer description and is something best practiced regularly before performing. I learned this tool some years ago in an acting class. It's called the walk-around. The underlying concept is that by allowing all our thoughts and emotions to just be, they eventually calm down and we can feel centered and ready to work. Initially, practice this at home, alone. Walking around in a large circle at a normal pace, you talk aloud and fill in the blanks of the following phrases with short answers—one word, if possible. The four blank phrases to fill in are: I Am, I Want, I Need, I Feel. Give yourself several times around for each blank, several answers, and then repeat, if you like. Do not edit yourself. Let it come out. You might contradict yourself; you might say crazy things. Do this walk-around for about five minutes at a time. Allowing all the thoughts and feelings to just be is similar to venting in a journal or any kind of good catharsis. The reason to do it walking and speaking aloud is to keep the mind from spinning off into myriad thoughts. A sample walk-around might start this way: I am a woman, I am mad, I am okay, I am crap, I am a musician, I am a wife, I am tired, I am blanking, I am anxious, I am nervous, I am okay. And so forth and so on. If you find that no words come out, you might just say, " I am blanking" and then go on to the next category. After some practice, attempt to make a real difference between the "I Want" and the "I Need." After *several weeks* of practice, you can attempt to just think it while you walk around backstage. By then you probably will have absorbed the technique enough that your mind will not wander. I have found this tool to be of amazing strength and help. I have used it backstage and at times of real crisis or difficulty in my daily life and it has helped me become calm, clear-headed, and focused.

Along with the kinds of preparation described above, prepare yourself physically. As mentioned in the previous section on performing, take care of yourself the way an athlete does. Make sure you get copious amounts of sleep, nourishing food and water, along with moderate exercise, because together these can go a long way toward building confidence and fighting nerves.

Wade in the shallow end of the pool, rather than dive off the diving board. When you know you have a big performance coming up, look for opportunities to sing beforehand. Having positive performing experiences helps to assure more—success does breed success and dealing with nerves does get easier with experience. Maybe you can gather some relatives and friends together in your living room and perform part of your upcoming program. When your teacher is giving a studio recital, and you are nervous about that event, perhaps your teacher would arrange for just a few of you to sing for each other as a practice. If you are planning on auditioning for college or graduate school, look into performing your audition program in advance. Are there several of you in your school or studio who are getting ready for such auditions? Can you arrange some miniperformances for each other, or even hold mock auditions to simulate the atmosphere? How about giving each other feedback, even creating a support group of sorts?

Some musicians like to take beta-blockers, but I would caution against taking any drugs for performance anxiety. Sometimes they can be drying or habit-forming. If the strategies listed here do not work, check out the books in the performance anxiety bibliography, research on the Internet, or ask around for workshops near you.

Realize that most people have periods in their lives or particular situations that bring out performance anxiety. You are *not* alone. Yet, if you struggle a great deal with performance anxiety and self-confidence most of the time, and you have read some books and tried some exercises and techniques, and your performance anxiety is not much improved, it would be wise to seek out professional help. In that case, performance anxiety is often one manifestation of some deeper issues. My own journey from crippling stage fright to helping others overcome performance anxiety took me through books, workshops, journaling, and psychotherapy. If you are ready to delve in, therapy is not only for those people with huge problems and wallets to match. Nearly all colleges and universities offer free or very low cost counseling services. Most cities have clinics that are free or have a sliding fee scale and many clergy are trained in social work or counseling and can offer their services for free. Ask around.

9

AUDITIONING

AUDITIONING FOR OPERA AND ORATORIO

I HAVE YET TO MEET THE SINGER who *loves* auditions. In spite of this, they can be more enjoyable if you look on them as miniperformances. In some situations you can get immediate feedback, but even if feedback is not available, you can think of each audition as another opportunity to test your mettle, to set some goals for yourself, rather than try to figure out what the adjudicators want and please them. Listed below are some tips to help make the whole process a bit easier.

Repertoire: What the Fach?

"Fach" is a German word meaning category, particularly of specialization. For example, in German, a computer expert is a Computer Fachman. The categories, or fächer in plural, came about to protect opera singers under a year-long contract with an opera house (the norm there) from being required to sing too many diverse roles and thereby straining their voices. There are several good books and Web sites (see Resources) that list both the German and American fächer—since there are differences. I won't go into great detail here, but simply list the various fächer and representative artists, in each case, going from lighter to heavier. It would be helpful to take the list and find recordings of the various artists, to begin to get a sense of the tone quality for each fach.

Soprano

Soubrette	Lucia Popp, Dawn Upshaw
Lyric coloratura	Kathleen Battle, Joan Sutherland
Dramatic coloratura	June Anderson, Ruth Ann Swenson
Full lyric soprano	Mirella Freni, Renee Fleming
Spinto soprano	Leontyne Price, Deborah Voigt
Dramatic soprano	Hildegard Behrens, Eva Marton
Wagnerian soprano	Gwyneth Jones, Birgit Nilsson

Mezzo

Lyric mezzo	Jennifer Larmore, Frederica von Stade
Dramatic mezzo	Marilyn Horne, Christa Ludwig
Dramatic alto	Dolora Zajick, Grace Bumbry
Alto	Florence Quivar, Kathleen Ferrier

Tenor

Buffo tenor	Peter Schreier, Gerhard Unger
Lyric tenor	Frank Lopardo, Stanford Olsen
Full lyric tenor	Fritz Wunderlich, Alfredo Kraus
Spinto tenor	Luciano Pavarotti, Placido Domingo
Heldentenor	Gary Lakes, Siegfried Jerusalem

Baritone

Lyric baritone	Hermann Prey, Gino Bechi
Kavalier baritone	Haken Hagegard, Thomas Allen
Verdi baritone	Sherrill Milnes, Leo Nucci
Helden baritone	Thomas Stewart, James Morris

Bass

Buffo bass	Franco Corena, Italo Tajo
Heavy buffo	Alexander Kipnis, Kurt Moll
Bass baritone	Simon Estes, Samuel Ramey
Basso cantabile	Matti Salminen, Ezio Pinza

It can take some time for a particular voice to settle into its fach, yet if you are doing some opera or graduate school auditions, you need to *begin* the process of discovering your fach. Your teacher is the first resource, but you might also ask several coaches. It is always a good rule of thumb to stay on the lighter side of things, especially until you have reached vocal maturity, which can be anywhere from your midtwenties to age thirty. For Wagnerian voices, it can be age forty to forty-five! Many coaches and directors have told me that they would far rather hear a larger voice singing easily and beautifully in lyric repertoire than hear that same voice trying to negotiate dramatic (heavy) material. You need to stay more or less within a given fach, not only for your own vocal health, but also to avoid confusion. If you are a lyric soprano who generally sings arias such as "O Mio Babbino Caro" or "Quando m'en vo" or "Juliet's Waltz" and you throw in a Wagnerian aria, your adjudicators will wonder what is going on. Are you genuinely confused about your fach or do you think that you will grow into Wagnerian repertoire later?

For graduate schools and opera auditions, work with your teacher, coaches, and accompanists on developing a package. Usually that means at least five arias, with one each in Italian, French, German, English, and a wildcard—something very modern or unusual. If your voice is at home singing Mozart, always include a Mozart aria. They generally showcase good technique and adjudicators love them.

For oratorio auditions, the adjudicators like to hear the various languages, but the emphasis is on era. You need an aria from the baroque era (usually from a Bach or Händel mass or oratorio), one from the classical era (normally from a Mozart or Haydn mass or oratorio), one from the romantic era (Schubert, Brahms, Mendelssohn oratorios or masses), and a modern era piece (works by Copland, Rutter, Bernstein, and so forth).

Clothes and Appearance

Get yourself an outfit or two that you wear for auditions *only*. That way you avoid panic on discovering there are food stains on your dry-clean-only outfit and the audition is only two hours away. It can also be a psychological help—your uniform, so to speak, which will help you look on your audition as simply doing your job and get you in the frame of mind to perform.

If you are a mezzo auditioning for a pants role, wear a nice pantsuit. Depending on the role, you might also wear boots. Otherwise, women should wear dresses. The adjudicators want to see someone in that role who looks, for the most part, quite feminine. A low heel is also a good idea. Wear your audition outfit to a lesson or coaching to see if you feel grounded in your shoes and can breathe and support well enough in your clothes. For men, a suit is best but a blazer or just a shirt and tie or even a turtleneck can be perfectly fine. If you can find eye-catching colors, all the better. Be careful that what you wear is memorable (e.g., "Let's have the gal in the bright red dress come to callbacks.") and not silly ("Can you believe the jungle-bird skirt? I don't think she's our leading lady!"). Stay away from religious jewelry. You never know what your adjudicator's sensitivities/prejudices might be. Overall, you need to look like a diva/divo in professional attire—not evening wear. No tuxes, sequins, rhinestones, and so forth. Dress as if you were invited for tea with the Queen of England.

Within the framework of professional and a bit conservative, find the cut and color that flatter you. Sometimes women like to show some cleavage or leg, but be conservative.

Arrive as well groomed as possible. For men, that means hair nicely done and off the face and any facial hair neatly trimmed. For women, it is time to "diva up"—you need to look the part of a glamorous singer—so wear some jewelry and well-applied makeup, just stay away from an evening look. As with men, be sure that your hair does not cover your face, because you need to communicate with your face, especially your eyes. If you are not accustomed to wearing makeup, get some help from friends, relatives, or teachers. Big department stores have makeup specialists who can help you in both selection and application.

Mechanics

There is usually someone back stage who will take your paperwork and announce you to the adjudicators. You are *now* on stage. This can be the most important part of the audition, when you show that you are genuinely friendly and warm. Smile and look right at them. When it feels appropriate, make a bit of small talk about the beautiful morning or whatever, but be careful to balance friendliness with professionalism. Let them lead the way in terms of shaking hands. Some like the contact; others would prefer to remain in the background.

As you are smiling and talking, you are also walking up on stage and greeting the accompanist. Now is the time to show him or her the unusual cuts or other variances from the printed score that you will take. Go to center stage and wait a moment. Usually the adjudicators will have your materials in front of them and will simply ask you what you would like to sing. If they do not, then announce yourself (not "My name is"—it sounds silly) and your piece: "Good Morning! I am Mary Sunshine and I will sing 'Quando m'en vo.'" Unless your aria is terribly obscure, you never need to give composers or titles of operas. Take a few moments to prepare and then focus slightly above their heads. Adjudicators like to be voyeurs in a sense and see you in performance. It is best not to look directly at them. Enjoy the opportunity to simply perform!

Always start with your strongest piece, even if the person ahead of you just nailed it. Your singing of it is still valid—it is *your* interpretation. Never try to second-guess adjudicators: "If I sing my *Fidelio* aria in German, maybe they won't ask for my Mozart aria, which is also in German and doesn't feel very good today." You never know. They just might ask for the Mozart. I tell students to warm up for their auditions by just starting each aria and then going with the one that feels best that day. The adjudicators may want to hear more, they may not, and they may even stop you. Contrary to what many singers think, none of these actions is necessarily indicative of how well you did. One stage director told me that she only asks for a second piece if the singer did so badly on the first that she wants to give him or her a second chance!

For oratorio auditions, the format is the same, but you use your score. You need to have two black binders of your package—one for you and one for the accompanist.

Professionalism

Always arrive at least twenty minutes early. Often there is paperwork to fill out and you may give yourself an edge if you can accommodate the adjudicators by going early when they have had a cancellation. No one wants to just sit around and they will be appreciative of your flexibility and cooperation. Arrive warmed up—especially in New York City, there is rarely an audition site with space for warming up. You can certainly lip-trill or hum lightly while you wait, but that may need to be in the bathroom so that you are not disrupting other auditions.

Networking helps singers, but at auditions, do it after you sing. Chatting with others can pull you off center and exacerbate performance anxiety because nervous chatter can have a snowball effect. And there *are* some unscrupulous folks who might try to undermine your confidence with prying questions or snide remarks. Smile at your colleagues, promise to catch up afterwards, and find some place to be alone, even if it is just facing a corner. Take some deep breaths and focus on how you would like to sound—visualize your performance. Breathing deeply through your nose will humidify the air, relax you a bit, and remind you where to track the resonance.

Bring your résumé and head shot, even if you have sent them ahead, because such things can get lost in the shuffle. Bring a black binder with your music copied front to back and all cuts and changes from the written score boldly and clearly marked. Even if you have sent materials ahead of time, it is a good idea to bring several copies of your aria list and your binder. Be prepared to sing something from the work they are presenting, if at all possible, but do not agree to sing something that you have not prepared. If they want to hear something new to you, suggest coming back at another time.

If the accompanist provided starts the tempo too fast or too slow, ask the adjudicators if you may start over and sing a few bars for the accompanist. Never snap your fingers—it is considered rude. Always thank your accompanist (that person is often the company's music director) and thank the adjudicators. Never apologize or show disappointment to anyone: the adjudicators, the accompanist, or singers waiting their turn. It can be so tempting to say, "I can sing this so much better. I'm sorry. May I try again?" Do not give in to such temptation—it is simply unprofessional and puts you in a weak position. Always play the part of the confident performer, even if you do not feel that way. Everyone has off-days and the adjudicators know that. By the same token, if you know you will not sing well because of illness, do not try to sing through it—cancel the audition. First impressions can be lasting.

When you need to cancel, do everything in your power to get word to them. If that means giving someone twenty dollars to take a note in, do it. The music world is *very* small and not showing up for an audition will stay with you—especially if it happens more than once, word will get around, and unless you are the next big star, no one will want to work with you.

Send a thank-you note afterward. So few people do this and it can show that you are thoughtful and willing to be part of a team. Your note could simply say, "Thank you for making time in your busy schedule to hear me sing. Best wishes for a wonderful season." It is also an opportunity to mention additional supportive information, such as "hearing today that you might change the scheduled opera from *Falstaff* to *Die Fledermaus*, I would like to let you know that I have sung the role of Adele with Pie in the Sky Opera Company and I would love the opportunity to perform it again."

Learning from the Process

When you can look on auditions as just another performance, another chance to test your mettle, you will, indeed, grow through the experience. One way to help you stay in the laboratory or experimental frame of mind is to keep a journal or log. You will be able to track patterns and to see what helps you perform at your best. For example, when I was in graduate school and singing many auditions, I found through log-keeping that it was very important for me to eat some protein the night before, to eat fruit or other light foods the day of the audition, to sing in the late morning or early afternoon if possible, and to get at least nine hours of sleep the night before. Some people are highly affected by the barometric pressure and other weather conditions, others by the acoustics of the audition space. Of course, you can tailor the log or journal to your needs and add categories not listed below.

Sample Log

Day, date and time of audition _____

School/company/program _____

Audition space/acoustics_____

Accompanist _____

Outfit worn _____

Any feedback _____

How I felt I did (percentage) _____ (comments) _____

_____

Emotional state beforehand _____

Physical state beforehand _____

How much sleep the night before _____

Food eaten the night before_____

Food eaten on audition day _____

The weather conditions _____

Other factors _____

(later) Results _____

MUSICAL THEATRE AUDITIONS

Much of the process is similar to opera in dress, supporting materials, behavior, and so forth. The difference is primarily in selecting repertoire. Musical theatre singers need to have many more songs that can easily be polished for auditions. Normally, you do not have a package as with opera that is constantly being polished and refined. Instead, you learn and perform (in studio recitals and performance classes) as many songs as possible from the following eras:

- Songs written prior to 1939 (Arlen, Berlin, Gershwin, Porter, Romberg, Sullivan, etc.)
- Songs written in the Golden Age 1940–60 (Lerner and Loewe, Rodgers and Hammerstein, Bernstein, Loesser, etc.)

- Songs written between 1960 and 1975 (Bock and Harnick, Kander and Ebb, Schmidt and Jones, etc.)
- Songs written from 1975 to the present (Yeston, Sondheim, Schwartz, Brown)

Then you choose audition repertoire depending on the show that will be presented and the character for which you would like to be considered. This is where your own research into the show, some coaching, and asking questions can help. Some directors like to hear songs from the show that will be presented; most do not. In opera, the technical requirements are usually higher, so adjudicators want to hear the major arias from a particular opera to see if the singer can handle them. In musical theatre, the danger is being dismissed from consideration. When you audition with the ingénue's song from the show and your appearance is vastly different from what the director had in mind, she or he probably will not consider you for other roles. A phone call to ascertain what the director would like to hear is essential. Then work with your teacher, coach, and accompanist to determine your strongest material. If, for example, you would like to be considered for a rather sultry character in a Sondheim musical, you might find a song from that musical or from another Sondheim work or you may choose to go with sultry material from another composer.

Generally you will be told how much material to prepare. Sometimes it is only sixteen bars; sometimes you are given five minutes to work with. Be sure you use the time to your advantage. With high notes as your specialty and only sixteen bars to sing, select from the music the highest section. If you have five minutes or so, include songs that show both the lowest and highest parts of your range. A frequent request is for contrasting material: an up-tempo song and a ballad. As you add to your repertoire, it would be wise to keep that in mind. Another contrast that adds to the audition is to have a comedic song as well as a love song. Keep these possibilities and the need to show off your range in mind as you peruse songbooks for material. Another consideration is characterization. The director Bob Fosse divided songs into three categories:

1. The "I Am" song—meaning it's a song in which the character reveals something about themselves.
2. The "I Want" song—meaning the character needs something and that need drives the song.
3. "New" which is every other type of song.

The strongest choices for auditions are from the first two categories. When chosen correctly, they force you to reveal something about the character in the song—making your acting and presentation equal partners with your singing. Directors are more likely to cast someone with good acting and singing rather than someone who can sing well but has neglected the development of acting/presentation.

As you expand your repertoire, be mindful of the range of ages and types you can play. Take into consideration how you look, how you sound, what your strengths are. You can then almost always match yourself with a character of the show you are auditioning for. Knowing your type and what character you would be good for makes it easier to select materials because the process becomes more specific.

For some auditions, you may need to have a monologue ready as well, and in this area, too, it is wise to have several selections ready. You could choose a short humorous monologue, a longer one that really takes the character on a journey, and maybe another which shows a wide range of emotions.

For the initial audition, dress and deportment are usually similar to operatic auditions. The difference is in callbacks. Again, get as much information prior to the callback as you can. Very often callbacks involve more dance and you need to know how to dress. Sometimes they involve more singing, but usually the focus is on dance and reading from the script.

AUDITIONING FOR COLLEGE OR GRADUATE SCHOOL

Please read the first part of this chapter because many of the suggestions and recommendations apply. The difference is a matter of degree— auditions for acceptance into collegiate programs are usually a bit more informal and relaxed. However, do your best to be as professional and prepared as you can because it will go a long way toward impressing your adjudicators.

Selecting a School

Talk to your voice teacher, to your high school choral director, to friends and relatives, search the Internet and get as much information as you can. If former graduates from your high school are studying voice, call or e-mail them for their impressions. It is prudent to give some thought to the kind of academic environment you will thrive in.

Some wonderful music making, learning, and teaching goes on in liberal arts colleges. You would certainly get a well-rounded education, which can be of great help not only to broaden you as a person and give you substance to bring to your performing, but also to provide training for money-making or career options along with the music. In small colleges students usually receive a great deal of individual attention and ample performing possibilities. Often you can request frequent recitals, form ensembles and chamber groups, and be as active as you desire. The downside of small-college education is lack of opportunity for big-scale productions (it can be rare for colleges to mount entire operas or musical theatre shows), and sometimes an insular provincialism. This, of course, varies from school to school.

Conservatories can be awfully exciting places. Everyone is focused on their craft, on their performing, and the energy of all this can help motivate and sustain a student's studies. The amount of individual attention can vary, depending on the size, programs, and policies of the conservatory. Many times the private teachers have active performing careers, which can help you with ideas, with contacts, with a little more panache on your résumé, and with inspiration. Often students have opportunities for participation as soloists with choirs and orchestras, musicals, opera scenes, and fully mounted productions. The downside of this kind of education is the flip side of the focus. It is exciting to devote oneself to one's music, but conservatory education is, by nature, narrow. Liberal arts education usually gets a token nod. Also, the benefits of having a teacher who is actively performing can be outweighed by having to miss lessons for several weeks because she or he is off singing in an opera, and then having several lessons in a row. Not all conservatories allow such things, because it can be detrimental to the students' development.

Music departments or schools within universities can vary, again, in terms of size, programs, and policies. Frequently they combine the best aspects of the other two kinds of schools: broad liberal arts background along with intense focus on performing. Large productions are common along with good research facilities and often well-known, established teachers. Many times students can find performance options in student-run cabarets and coffeehouses and in departments or schools outside of the music program. These benefits can be outweighed by intense competition for opportunities, being closed out of desired classes, and often a greater amount of bureaucracy. If you feel lost in dealing with red tape, if you want a lot of individual attention, a large university would not be a good situation for you.

Selecting a Teacher

After giving some thought to the kind of academic environment you would like, research potential teachers as well. Ask your voice teacher, your choral director, your friends, your relatives, and search the Internet for teachers in the various schools you are considering. You need to find both a good program match and a good fit with a teacher. The ideal situation, if your budget and schedule allow, would be to have a private lesson with the teacher before applying to the school. That person can advise you as to whether that particular school would be a good place for you. If the two of you work well together, and there is a great deal of competition to be accepted into the school, the teacher can sometimes pull some strings and make it easier for you to be accepted.

Audition Repertoire

Most colleges, conservatories, and universities list on their Web sites or their application materials the number and kind of pieces required for auditions. For undergraduates, it is usually two to three songs, with at least one in English and one in Italian. Here is where many young people err: they mistakenly believe that they will be impressive if they bring in more advanced material such as arias or songs in French or German. It is far more impressive to sing beginning songs, such as "Caro mio ben" with beautiful technique and expression than to bring in repertoire that is suitable for a more mature singer. Sometimes schools intentionally ask for simpler material to enable the adjudicators to focus on the singer's technique and evaluate whether that singer is ready for college-level work. When you bring in something difficult and do not sing it with ease, you will leave a poor impression.

For graduate students, most schools like to hear both art songs and arias. Be careful that you do not focus only on your arias. Just as adjudicators like to hear simple songs from potential undergraduates in order to evaluate their technique, so, too, do they like to hear art songs from potential graduate students. Unless you are a coloratura who just has to show off her high Fs by singing the "Queen of the Night" aria, you will be more impressive if you sing a simple, slow, sustained art song with fine technique and expression.

Supporting Materials

Singers need to be careful about supporting materials. Students auditioning for graduate school should bring an audition list, a repertoire list, a résumé, and perhaps a headshot to their auditions. This is not the case for undergraduates unless the school specifically asks for them. Bring these materials, if you have them, but wait to be asked for them and do not offer them to your adjudicators. The impression left by doing so is of someone overeager, perhaps even pushy, who may not be able to take direction and relearn some aspects of singing. Adjudicators are looking for talent and musicality, to be sure, but also for openness, flexibility, and even pliability. The majority of students, when starting collegiate vocal study, must relearn aspects of singing—especially technique. When a singer comes into an undergraduate audition singing difficult repertoire and offering all kinds of supportive material, the adjudicators usually believe that the singer conceives of him- or herself as a complete package and will not be able to start anew.

Information

Get as much information about the audition as you can. The admissions office and departmental secretary can usually answer most questions or conceivably you could be referred to a voice teacher or graduate student. Many singers have been thrown off center by not knowing, for example, that they have only ten minutes to go over repertoire with the provided accompanist or that instead of singing in a large, reverberating hall, they are auditioning for only two adjudicators in a dry classroom. Therefore ask and mentally prepare yourself for whatever the circumstances may be. If your questions are not answered, or you are shuffled from person to person, or someone makes you feel that you are imposing by asking for information, then marshal your support system. Could a parent, older sibling, voice teacher, or school advisor make some calls on your behalf? It is that important: being able to prepare yourself mentally can make the difference in the audition.

Some questions to ask are:

1. Is an accompanist provided? Do I have rehearsal time with the accompanist?
2. Is there warm-up space available?
3. Where will I be singing? Is it a large or small space?
4. For how many adjudicators will I be singing?
5. How is the audition conducted? Do I select my first piece or do they?
6. Are audition lists, repertoire lists, and résumés required?
7. When will I be notified of the audition results?
8. Are there teachers or admissions personnel who can answer questions that day?

Good luck!

CHORAL AUDITIONS

Nearly all community, church, and temple choir auditions are more relaxed than the kind of auditions just discussed. Sometimes the director simply vocalizes the singer and asks him or her to sight-read some music. It would be sensible to telephone or e-mail in advance and ask if a prepared piece is required. If so, a short selection from an oratorio in English is often a good choice, but do ask the director.

If you are in a choir and would like to be considered for solo opportunities, approach the director with a list of choral solos you have learned and prepared with your voice teacher. Be aware that it may take some time for him or her to give you an audition and to consider you as a soloist. It can be a challenge to rise from the ranks, as it requires a shift in how you are perceived. If possible, get some solo credits with other groups and inform your director via letter, e-mail, or résumé of that experience.

For professional choirs, a formal audition is usually mandatory. A complete oratorio package, formal dress, and so forth, as discussed earlier, would be necessary. Practice sight singing as much as you can, for that is often an important part of choral auditions.

Good luck!

10

SINGING AS A CAREER OR AVOCATION

DON'T DO IT ALONE: NETWORKING
IN HIGH SCHOOL, COLLEGE, AND BEYOND

ANYONE CAN NETWORK in high school, college, or at anytime. You do not have to be aggressive in any way. It simply means letting people in your daily life know that you are studying singing and that you would enjoy opportunities to perform. What *could* stand in the way of networking would be trying to live out a Hollywood-style fantasy: let no one know that you are learning to sing until you have reached a professional level and then suddenly burst on the scene and amaze everyone. Despite what you might see on TV reality shows, that *is* a fantasy. Most singers slowly. build their technique, their performing skills, and their singing careers. For a truly professional level of technique, that process usually requires from five to seven years of study, along with diligent practice, listening, reading, and so forth. Since it is a process, why not let people in your life know what is going on with you? For example, you tell your hairstylist about taking voice lessons; the stylist remembers that some months from now and asks if you are available to sing at a cousin's wedding. That is often how people get singing jobs, or any kind of freelance work: through word of mouth. What can take some of the fear out of networking is that it truly is just sharing information and the sharing is often reciprocal. When you are happy with that hairstylist you would be likely to recommend her or him when asked for a referral by a friend.

Occasionally you will meet singers who believe that since there is a finite number of performing/singing opportunities, it is best to keep the knowledge of openings to oneself. That will likely backfire. The music world is very small and selfishness and hoarding behavior will eventually be noticed, negatively. No one singer can fill all the needs, so why not share information on auditions and performing opportunities? The adage "what goes around comes around" is apt here. At a time when you have a scheduling conflict and cannot sing for a wedding or some other engagement, and you pass that opportunity on to another singer, chances are that this person will send work your way when she or he has a scheduling conflict.

In high school, be sure that your teachers (especially music teachers), your guidance counselor, and even your principal know about your voice studies. If you attend church or temple, offer to sing at services for free and do the same for your scout or PTA meeting. That valuable experience can later be turned into a money-making activity. Along the way, check with your teacher about your readiness for performing. Low key opportunities such as church, temple, or short performances at meetings of service organizations (Kiwanis, Rotary, etc.) can actually help your technical growth as well as your performing skills. When your teacher feels you are ready for more, read the next part of this chapter for ideas on how to make singing pay and explore the possibility of using your talent to help pay for college. Many colleges and universities offer scholarships—some without the requirement of majoring in music. Often service organizations have auditions or competitions for scholarships and you can check out national-level possibilities through *Classical Singer* and the National Association of Teachers of Singing (NATS) journal If you plan to major in music, compare notes with other students planning the same. You might be able to share information on the best teachers at certain colleges or exchange admissions interview strategies. Maybe you could even be each other's support system and share the costs of campus visits and auditions.

In college or university, ask your teacher about your readiness level and what performances might be possible. A subscription to *Classical Singer* would be a help, as would joining music fraternities, student chapters of NATS, and the Music Educators National Conference (MENC). If your school does not have such organizations, you and your colleagues could start one! Certainly let your roommates, your suite mates, and your dorm mates know of your interest and availability to perform, as well as professors and campus clergy. Check kiosks, campus newspapers, and departmental bulletin boards for performing opportunities. In all your activities, network not only for performing possibilities but also for information. There is no better way to discover the best teachers, coaches, and directors than to compare notes with fellow singers. Other than choral and operatic/theatrical activities, singing can be a lonely experience because singers must spend a great deal of time alone, practicing and studying. The more you can connect with other singers, the friendlier the whole experience will be. It is also valuable to simply share ideas, concepts, frustrations, and worries. In fact, a great deal of any student's education happens *outside* of classes. I certainly learned as much from talking with and observing my colleagues in graduate school as I did from formal classes. Get connected and stay connected for the information, the opportunities, the support, and the fun!

Once you have finished with college or graduate school, the networking does not end. Now it is even more important to have up-to-date materials (see the previous section) and to get the word around, whether it is for teaching or performing. Keeping active in your college or university's alumni association, and any musical organizations is the first step. Be sure to check out local chapters of NATS (whether you teach or perform), the national NATS, MENC national and local chapters, and any other local organizations. When you are in need of funds for your development, whether as a performer or teacher, consult with your colleagues and your circle of friends. Perhaps you know of a wealthy individual who might be able to fund, say, an audition trip? In that case, it usually works best to avoid asking directly for money, as that puts the person on the spot and usually makes for an uncomfortable encounter. What can help is to simply ask him or her for ideas. Sometimes they may have other people to recommend, they might offer to approach others on your behalf, they might suggest you perform a fund-raising concert in their spacious home, or they may ask "How much do you need?" and write you a check. Asking for advice puts him or her on your side as part of your team, rather than a distant entity from whom you want something.

No matter what kind of singing work interests you, keep a file folder, computer file, or a notebook of contacts. When you are in a show and given a contact list for the cast, hold onto it. You may need to contact someone for advice or assistance in the future. Keep contact information for all your gigs as you might need to ask for letters of reference or testimonials. Keep accurate lists of any mailings you have done both for future approaches and to avoid duplication.

PAYBACK TIME: MAKING MONEY WITH YOUR VOICE

Check with your teacher about your readiness for work and when you are given the okay, there are several avenues to explore.

If you are in college or graduate school, find out whether your school has a career center where you can leave your résumé and contact information for possible jobs at weddings, funerals, bar/bat mitzvahs, and banquets. Keep your contact information up to date.

Many large churches and temples hire soloists or section leaders for their choirs and Catholic parishes are often in need of cantors. This kind of work can be an especially good match for a student, because the working hours are usually on the weekends (although some do have midweek rehearsals). Another advantage to church and temple work is the possibility of being asked to do weddings, funerals, and bar/bat mitzvahs, not to mention the social benefit. In addition to information from your teacher or your school's career center, check your local paper's Sunday classifieds. Alternatively, do a direct mailing. Go through the yellow pages or do an Internet search for area churches and temples, then send the organist/choir director a brief cover letter and your résumé You might specify that you are looking for section leader work or for singing at funerals or other special services. Many temples hire soloists or section leaders for the High Holy Days and a mailing for that work should be done at least six months in advance. Send your materials to the cantor.

Check your local paper's classifieds for stage opportunities as well as church/temple. You might be surprised at the number of auditions for concerts and plays. For opera (including apprentice programs and chorus openings), oratorio, and church/temple work, you might consider a subscription to *Classical Singer*. As a subscriber, you can utilize their Web site for up-to-date listings (http://www.classicalsinger.com). For information on musical theatre auditions, consider a subscription to *Back Stage* or *Back Stage West*. Again, subscribers can access audition announcements on their Web site: http://www.backstage.com.

If you have the time and the opportunity to audition for a chorus role in a production that requires union membership, jump at it! Union affiliation can give your résumé some clout and provide you with low-cost insurance and other benefits. The three most important unions for singers also have Web sites with all kinds of information, including auditions. The catch is that you have to be hired in a union show in order to join. The three main unions that cover singers and actors are:

- American Guild of Musical Artists (AGMA): http://www.musical-artists.org
- American Federation of Television and Radio Artists (AFTRA): http://www.aftra.org
- Actors Equity Association (AEA): http://www.actorsequity.org

Another possible direct mailing would be to wedding planners, halls that are rented for weddings and receptions, and bridal shops. In this mailing, include several business cards, a brief letter, your résumé, and a brochure, if you have one. When people have praised you for your performance at their events, approach them later with a reference request. If they are willing to jot down a line or two, you can prepare a list of reviews to send out to potential clients and use in mass mailings. Otherwise, a list of satisfied customers and their phone numbers or e-mail addresses would be a strong endorsement as well as helping you to obtain more singing work.

Try a mass mailing to community choruses, not only to be considered for oratorio soloist openings but also as a "ringer" (a trained singer brought in at the last minute to beef up a section). Try an Internet search for sites in your area that are devoted to choruses.

Many community arts organizations have funds for recitals and concerts. Consideration may involve a formal review process, or it might be as simple as making a brief proposal along with supporting materials. You can start the inquiry with a phone call, letter, or Internet search. You could also send your materials to local orchestras with suggestions of works featuring voice and orchestra.

Singers often ask, "When do I approach an agent or manager?" The answer is, when you have something to manage. It is a fantasy to think that someone who has the whole package (beautiful voice, expressive performing, good looks) will be taken under the wing of an agent who will scour the world for performance opportunities and make a career happen. While that may very occasionally be true, management generally wants to work with a known quantity. Often singers under management continue to do most of the work of finding opportunities. Their being under management simply gives them a bit more clout and opens some auditions to them. Because this book is intended for the amateur and the student, a lengthy discussion of management is better left to books aimed at the emerging professional. Suffice it to say that your first task is to get as much performing under your belt as possible. Once you have had a series of paid performances and the likelihood of more, consult some of the books in the Resources section for help in how to approach management.

Classical Singer has featured articles in many issues about creating your own performance opportunities, especially in schools. It would be worthwhile looking through their archives. A few suggestions might include creating a song recital of works that would have been heard during our country's formative years or during the Civil War, and sending a mailing to schools, concert series, and museums offering this artistic and educational program. You could create programs around all kinds of themes ranging from American composers to women composers to songs based on Shakespeare's texts to songs about animals, and so on.

Perhaps you could find another singer or an instrumentalist to team up with. Creating your own performance opportunities is a fair amount of work, requiring skills of promotion, organization, and finance as well as musicianship and artistry. The rewards are also great, and you will be in control of programming, scheduling, and venue. Good luck!

PROFESSIONALISM: BUSINESS CARDS, RÉSUMÉS, AND PICTURES—WHAT, WHEN, AND WHY

It can be so tempting (and fun) to start amassing the trappings of a busy singer. Unless you have money to burn, be judicious in your acquisition of promotional materials. Check with teachers and coaches about what you need and when. You do not want to miss opportunities because you lack the appropriate materials, neither do you need everything at once. Certainly begin with a résumé and a business card and wait until those generate income or opportunities before you acquire other tools.

Business Cards

In your arsenal of supporting materials, business cards will probably be the first item. When you are asked to sing at weddings or other events on a regular basis, or you would like to create such activities, a business card with your name, voice type, phone number, and e-mail address will be a useful tool. You can have them made at a print shop or make your own. Most computers have software templates for business cards and office supply stores carry the card stock. Buy an inexpensive card case and carry it with you always—you might be surprised how often the situation will arise when someone will ask for your card. You can keep the cards offered in exchange from other folks—again, this can come in handy for all kinds of networking.

Résumé

If you are in high school, chances are you do not need a résumé In fact, as mentioned in the chapter on auditioning, it can actually work against you in some college audition situations. Nonetheless, it would be wise to keep track of your activities and start a résumé for later use. If you are in college or graduate school, you will need a résumé for school applications, apprentice applications, and auditions. There are several books (see "Resources") that treat the development of a singer's résumé in depth, particularly for the aspiring professional. I will simply provide an overview here and a few samples. Give some thought to what you want the résumé to do for you, as it truly is a marketing tool. In looking for recital work, oratorio work, and singing for weddings, funerals, bar/bat mitzvahs and other events, your résumé will be set up differently from the style you would use when looking for opportunities in opera and musical theatre.

- Make sure that your contact information is at the top. Your name, voice type, address, phone number, e-mail address and fax number need to be clearly indicated. You can set up the résumé in many styles, with all of the contact information centered or with it on the left side and personal information on the right. If your focus is musical theatre or opera, you need to list height, weight, hair and eye color.
- The overall layout is usually organized as follows: contact information, primary experiences, secondary experiences, training, honors, and special skills. If you are looking for musical theatre opportunities, then the sung roles you have performed would be primary and spoken plays or other musical activities, such as concerts could be secondary. If you are looking for opera, include scenes you have performed in as well as full-length operas.
- Some schools and employers are real sticklers about dates, wanting to be certain that the singer has been active, without big holes in his or her history, while others do not care that much. A young singer with consistent activity and an increasing amount of performing can use the dates advantageously. If you are older or had to stop singing for a while, you can leave off dates, but be prepared to be asked about your history. Each credit you list should include the role, the show or the opera, the conductor, stage director, place, and date. For recitals, list the venue and date.
- You can arrange material within a category by date or by importance. If you had a high-profile gig, but it was two years ago, it still might be wise to list it first.
- The top section and bottom section of the résumé tend to draw the reader's eye. Put the most important things there. When your experience is rather slim because you are young or in school but you have studied with well-known teachers, coaches, or directors, put that first and then your experience.
- Your résumé needs to be clear and readable with a lot of white space. You do not need to list every single thing you have ever been in—choose the most important. If you are looking for opera employment, list that first. Oratorio work, recitals, and other concerts can be listed, but summarize and list them as secondary experiences. The reader needs to know your focus.

- The training section can include earned degrees or simply your voice teachers, coaches, and directors. Include any organizations or affiliations, especially if you are a member of a musicians' or actors' union.
- If you have received music scholarships or awards or won contests and competitions, list these in the honors and skills section. You can also list languages you have studied, instruments you play, dance styles you have learned, and any other skills, such as juggling, martial arts, and so forth.
- When your goal is to be the most active wedding, funeral, bar/bat mitzvah singer in your area, your résumé still needs to feature concert appearances. A listing of weddings and other such events is possible, but as its own document, never as part of a résumé.

Below are some sample résumés. The first is a mezzo soprano. Our mezzo is a high-school senior looking to realize further opportunities in theatre and planning to major in music and theatre in college. Therefore, she doesn't have as much training and as many special skills to list as our next résumé that belongs to a college student. She is savvy, though, in her listing of credits. It is not always the most recent performance that is listed first, but the more important. Accordingly being in community theatre is higher level than high school productions, and singing as soloist with an all-county chorus is more prestigious than performing with one's own high school chorus.

MEREDITH MEZZO
Mezzo Soprano

440 Melody Lane			Height: 5'7"	
Tuneful, CA 94102			Weight: 140	
415-234-5678			Hair: Light Brown	
meredithmezzo@aol.com			Eyes: Olive	

Theatre

Jekyll & Hyde	Emma	Chatham Players	C. Thestage, Dir.	2003
How to Succeed. . .	Ms. Jones	Script & Cue	C. Thelights, Dir.	2002
Alice in Wonderland	Alice	Tuneful High School	S. Easy, Dir.	2004
Fiddler on the Roof	Shprintze	Tuneful High School	A. Bow, Dir.	2005

Concerts

Mendelssohn *Elijah*	Soloist	Bay-wide Chorus	A. Armwaver	2004
Mozart *Requiem*	Soloist	Tuneful High Chorus	A. Armwaver	2005

Honors and Awards
San Francisco All-Girls Chorus, 2003–05
Recipient, Tuneful Kiwanis Club Scholarship for Voice Lessons 2003–05

Training

Voice:	Melody Lerner	Dance:	Johnny Onhistoes
Acting:	Tuneful Youth Theatre Workshops	Piano:	O. B. Nimble

In the résumé below, our soprano is finishing her college years with a very good amount of performance experience under her belt. She has been active in performances in her school, in summer programs, and in outside venues. Because her performances are at a higher level, they can speak for themselves and she does not list the directors. That is a personal choice. The reason to list directors, voice teachers, and other professionals is to make connections with adjudicators or potential employers. The music world is very small and connections often help in making the unknown person into a known quantity or giving that person a bit more élan. Even though our soprano has actually done more concert/oratorio work than opera, she lists opera first and also lists roles she has studied but not yet performed. That lets the reader know immediately that opera singing is her main goal. Notice the difference in titles of the operas. Listing it as *The Magic Flute* rather than *Die Zauberflöte* tells the reader that the opera was sung in English. And noting her participation in *Le Nozze di Figaro* rather than *The Marriage of Figaro* makes it clear the work was sung in Italian. She has a union affiliation from her chorus stint in *The Marriage of Figaro* for a professional company. That is rare for someone her age. Sondra has won a scholarship and "placed" in competitions—always a good thing to include. She also has several skills, including playing instruments, dance training, and Yoga.

SONDRA SOPRANO
Lyric Coloratura
AGMA
150 West 120th Street, #6E
New York, NY 10025
(212) 345-6789
FAX: (212) 345-6788
sondrasoprano@earthlink.net

Operatic Experience

Queen of the Night	*The Magic Flute*	Juilliard Opera	2005
Susanna	*Nozze di Figaro*	Juilliard Opera	2004
Juliet	*Roméo et Juliette*	Aspen Music Festival	2004
Miss Wordsworth	*Albert Herring*	Aspen Music Festival	2004
Norina	*Don Pasquale*	Bel Canto Opera	2003
Chorus	*Marriage of Figaro*	Opera West	2005

Roles Prepared

Oscar	*Un Ballo in Maschera*
Zerlina	*Don Giovanni*
Adina	*L'Elisir d'Amore*

Concert Experience

Mass in C Minor	Mozart	New York Choral Society	2005
Exultate, Jubilate	Mozart	Chamber Orchestra of New York	2005
Requiem	Mozart	Juilliard Choral Society	2004
The Creation	Haydn	New York Choral Society	2004
Mass in B Minor	Bach	New York Choral Artists	2003
Messiah	Händel	Juilliard Choral Society	2003
Magnificat	Bach	Masterworks Chorale	2003

Awards and Contests

Finalist: American Opera Auditions, 2005
Finalist: Metropolitan Opera Auditions Regional, New York District, 2004
Scholarship and Fellowship in Opera, Juilliard School

Education

Bachelor of Music, The Juilliard School, 2006
Teachers: Barry Tone, Hi Range
Coaches: Joan Attakeys, Will Play, Ima Singers Frend

Languages

Fluent French, Italian; Basic German, Spanish

Special Skills

Piano, Harp, Jazz, Tap, Ballet, certified Yoga instructor

Our baritone is a first-year conservatory student interested in a career in theatre. He has started his academic career well, having been cast in the ensemble of two works. Again, they have more importance than leading roles done in high school, so they are listed first. The same goes for being in the ensemble of a community theatre, hence the order of his list. Barry has left off his address, because he is in a dorm and it will change often, whereas his cell phone and e-mail address will not. Although still young, his special skills entries are interesting. He appears accomplished, with fluency in a foreign language and skill at playing two instruments along with fencing. The note about clowning is interesting and might make for a good conversation starter.

BARRY BARITONE
Baritone

| 617-789-9012 (cell) | | Height: 5'11" | Weight 160 |
| barrybaritone@msn.com | | Eyes: blue | Hair: black |

THEATRE

H.M.S. Pinafore	Ensemble	Boston Conservatory	2005
Seven Deadly Sins	Ensemble	Boston Conservatory	2005
Kiss Me, Kate	Ensemble	Foxboro Theatre	2004
Carousel	Billy Bigelow	Foxboro High School	2004
Annie Get Your Gun	Frank Butler	Foxboro High School	2005
The Mousetrap	Giles Ralston	Foxboro High School	2003

CONCERTS

| Soloist | Fauré *Requiem* | Foxboro High School Chorus | 2005 |
| Chorus | Duruflé *Requiem* | All State Chorus at Carnegie Hall | 2004 |

EDUCATION AND TRAINING
Student at The Boston Conservatory, majoring in Musical Theatre
Voice: Stan Tall, E.Z. Resonance
Acting: Faind Ureself, South Shore Conservatory Actor's Workshop

HONORS AND AWARDS
All State Solo and Ensemble, 1st place 2003, 2005
Talent Scholarship, Foxboro Rotary Club
Freshman Scholarship, The Boston Conservatory

SPECIAL SKILLS
Piano, Guitar, fluent Spanish, Clowning, Fencing

Our tenor is a high school junior, hoping to major in music in college. He has a great start with voice and piano lessons, lots of choral work, and even some opera experience. He could probably "pad" his résumé with all kinds of nonessentials. Leaving it honest and short and full of white space will actually serve him well. He has made some good choices, he has already done some solo work and this will be much stronger than a résumé full of every little thing he can think of.

TERRANCE TENOR
Tenor
10 Revere Lane
Chicago, IL 60625
(773) 345-6789
Atenor505@yahoo.com

Opera

Piquillo	Offenbach	*La Perichole*	Chicago Youth Opera Workshop	2004
Ensemble	Bizet	*Carmen*	Castle Hill Opera, Aurora	2005

Concerts

Soloist	Bach	*Magnificat*	Greater Chicago Youth Chorale	2004
Soloist	Dvořák	*Requiem*	Masterworks Youth Chorale	2004
Chorister	Beethoven	*9th Symphony*	Masterworks Youth Chorale	2003

Ensemble Participation

St. Andrew Choral Society, 2004–05
Revere Lane High School Chamber Choir, 2003–05
Revere Lane High School Select Chorus, 2002–05

Training

Voice: Carrie Atune   **Piano:** Strecha Atenotes
Fine Arts Summer Camp, Northwestern University 2003, 2004

Our next résumé is a recent college graduate looking for church, temple, wedding, funeral, and bar/bat mitzvah work. Because of that specific focus, it is set up differently from one aimed at concert and theatrical opportunities. He has certainly been active during his college years in Protestant, Catholic, and Jewish services. Note, however, that specific wedding, funeral, bar/bat mitzvah credits are not listed, but he offers references and testimonials.

WILL SINGFERYEW
Tenor
440 Songbird Lane, Apt. 1
Atlanta, GA 30021
(880) 321-9876
willsing@juno.com
http://www.willsing.com

Church and Temple Experience

Section Leader	Calvary Presbyterian Church	Alpharetta, GA	2001–present
Cantor (substitute)	St. Mary's Church	Atlanta, GA	2003–present
Soloist (quartet)	Temple Beth El	Atlanta, GA	2004–05

Oratorio Experience

Evangelist	Bach, *St. Matthew Passion*	Georgia State University	2005
Soloist	Bach, *Weihnachts Oratorium*	Buckhead Oratorio Society	2004
Soloist	Händel, *Messiah*	Calvary Presbyterian Church	2004
Soloist	Haydn, *Creation*	Calvary Presbyterian Church	2003

Training

Bachelor of Music, Voice Performance	Georgia State University	2005
Master of Music, Voice Performance	Georgia State University	in progress
Voice: Tessie Toorah, Willyew Singwell		

Repertoire List, References, and Testimonials Available Upon Request

Our final sample résumé is of a well-trained, highly experienced amateur. Sophie Soprano started lessons as an adult and applied herself diligently. She is happy in her career in freelance software design and does not want to pursue music full time. She is an independent contractor so she can set her own hours, and she is free to pursue a wide range of performing opportunities. Sophie was a history minor (computer science major) in college and loves researching and putting together historic art song recitals.

Sophie Soprano
Lyric Soprano
456 Morningside Drive
Austin, TX 78711
(512) 345-6789
FAX: (512) 345-7890
sophiesoprano@hotmail.com
http://www.sophiesoprano.com

Recitals

Women on Both Sides: *Songs of the Civil War*

Houston Historical Society	October 2005
University of Texas at Austin Alumni Luncheon	May 2005
Austin Public Library Concert Series	November 2004
St. David's Episcopal Church (Austin) Recital Series	June 2004

Songs and Stories of the Old Southwest (with storyteller Blaine Trooth)

San Antonio River Walk Summer Festival	July 2004
San Antonio Public Library Concert Series	April 2004
Austin Public Schools Arts in the Classroom Project	October 2003

Cycles of a Woman's Life in Song and Poetry

St. David's Episcopal Church (Austin) Recital Series	May 2003
University of Texas at Austin: AAUW Meeting	March 2003
The Bookshelf Bookstore Recital Series (Austin)	November 2002
Austin Public Library Year of the Woman Concert Series	September 2002

Art Song Recital	St. David's Episcopal Church (Austin)	April 2002
Lieder Abend	Goethe Institut (Houston)	December 2001
Studio Recitals	(Support and Tuneful studios)	1999–2001

Oratorio Experience

Soprano Soloist	Händel, *Messiah*	Austin Oratorio Society	December 2004
Soprano Soloist	Haydn, *Creation*	San Antonio Oratorio	April 2003
Soprano Soloist	Bach, *Magnificat*	Austin Oratorio Society	December 2002

Training

Voice: O.B. Tuneful, Ken U. Support   Coaching: Phil Maebeat

B.S. University of Texas at Austin: Major: Computer Science, Minor: American History

References, Reviews and Concert Proposals Available Upon Request

Headshots

Headshots can be expensive, but for someone trying to build a career or even a steady sideline, they are a good investment. Until the student is a collegiate junior, senior, or graduate student, they are usually unnecessary. Because they are an investment, shop around. Have you seen photos of colleagues that are effective? Find out who the photographer is. Are you at a loss for ideas? Check out the listings in *Backstage* and *Classical Singer*. Take the time to view the photographer's portfolio before you decide. Some colleges and universities have student photographers who are quite skilled. That might be a more affordable first step. In that case, you may want to be highly experimental and not go through all the steps listed below. If, however, you are going with a professional photographer, your cash outlay will be more substantial and it would be wise to prepare for your session.

Since there are resources that cover headshots in some detail, I will simply outline the basics here.

- First, look through Musical America's *International Directory of the Performing Arts* in a good music library, books listed in the "Resources" section, and your colleagues' head shots to get ideas for dress, jewelry, poses, and the like.
- Avoid photographers who do a lot of generic work and portraits. You need someone who knows what works for a headshot and knows what the music business is looking for. You also need to be able to rely on him or her to give you feedback about your overall look.
- Hire a professional makeup/hair artist. The photographer will likely be able to recommend people she or he works with on a regular basis. If not, ask around. This step is essential for women but men can also have their image enhanced this way.
- Your clothes should be neat, clean, and elegant but in no way distract from your face. Solid colors are best. If you are in doubt about

what looks best, ask a singer friend's advice and take several outfits to the shoot to get the photographer's feedback. Concert attire is often a good choice, although some men look very good in a simple turtleneck.

- Women, take some interesting jewelry—especially earrings. As with auditions, avoid religious jewelry. Men, you probably should leave off earrings in a formal headshot.
- If your shoot is in the morning, be sure to arise early. That will allow any puffiness in the face to drain.
- Headshots generally fall into one of two types: open and friendly or dramatic and intense. Scheduling and paying for a long shoot will allow you to try many kinds of looks. Otherwise, practice in front of a mirror and ask friends for feedback. If both looks work for you, you might want to have two headshots. One would be the intense, serious artist look to be reproduced in programs. The open, friendly look would be ideal for sending along with other materials to schedule auditions. It would help give the impression that you are someone who is easy to work with.

Demo CDs, Brochures, and Web Sites

These can be effective tools, but again, I would say more useful for a graduate student or emerging professional. Recording costs can be quite high and until your technique is secure and reliable and your voice has settled—which often does not happen until mid- to late twenties—you will be spending a lot of money for something you will not use for long. The quality of your voice will keep changing and the kinds of repertoire and the ranges involved will change until your voice has settled. Once you have paid for a good demo, it would be wise to use it for several years. If you need to make a recording in order to apply for college, graduate study, or some special program, do some research on microphones and computers. You need to have the highest quality available to you, because you cannot rely on the listeners being able to distinguish between your abilities and the overall quality of the recording. There are some inexpensive solutions like the Griffin™ imic™ which plugs a microphone into a computer's USB port. There are also some software products available for recording, some of them affordable. Check with computer and electronics stores.

Brochures and other printed material are usually reserved for ensembles and groups. An exception would be if you have several packaged or themed recitals or concerts polished and ready to offer. In that case, you would want to promote yourself to different libraries and service organizations and other venues, and a brochure might be of value to you.

Another possibility would be making a brochure to promote yourself as a wedding/funeral/bar/bat mitzvah singer. Until you have enough gigs to justify the print shop and the designer, do the work yourself on a computer and photocopier.

Web sites are also a good tool and I know many young people have fun creating and designing their own. For promotion, however, they need to look very polished and you may consider waiting until you have the funds to hire a professional. In the meantime, *Classical Singer* magazine/website offers inexpensive hosting and site building.

11

PHILOSOPHY OF SINGING

SOME MUSINGS ON THE PSYCHOLOGY OF SINGING

MAKE NO MISTAKE ABOUT IT—singing takes courage! Some of the reasons for that are:

1. Singers are both the instrument and the player. Unable to put the instrument back in its case and leave it in the corner, a singer must carry it around, exposing it to changes of temperature, humidity, barometric pressure, and all the current viruses. This instrument is affected not only by atmospheric changes but also by food, amount of sleep and emotional states. Singers must use their instruments in daily communication and often find difficulty in being as quiet as they would like before a performance.
2. Singers cannot hear their own voices accurately. They hear themselves through bones that conduct most of the sound to the ears, and in doing so, the sound is distorted. Singers have to go more by body sensations and even those can be elusive. They must learn (and teach) without being able to see the instrument and the technique involved! Think how well that would work with piano or violin!
3. Singing is more than mere pitches and rhythms. Classical singers must become familiar with several foreign languages, singing with diction as perfect as a native speaker. Singers must understand and communicate the poetry as well as the music, and incorporate acting—even if only in the face. All this must be done from memory and without an instrument to hide behind.

4. Singing is, quite simply, the most vulnerable of the performing arts. One bares one's soul in singing and performing well. Many singers hide behind bravura, diva-fits, ultracompetitiveness or plain denial. Others turn to vices. Ever wondered why so many singers are overweight? Most other methods of escape (drugs, alcohol, and smoking) interfere with singing—food usually does not.

All right, so singing is a challenge, but you love it, or you would not even try. So how do we deal with the difficulty and vulnerability inherent in singing? Here are some suggestions:

Give yourself a break! Especially when you are in transition from one technique to another or from one voice type to another, be kind to yourself. When you practice, avoid listening to yourself, at least the first few times you try a given exercise. Look on your practice time as a laboratory situation: step outside yourself and see what works and what does not. Just as you would probably give yourself several attempts at swinging a golf club or shooting a basket before critiquing yourself, give yourself several tries at a hard passage or new exercise or new aspect of technique. Try treating yourself in your practice sessions as if you were teaching someone else. You would undoubtedly use affirming language, not the negative self-talk that fills so many practice rooms.

Take care of your inner life. Practice your faith, whatever it is. Learn some Yoga or Tai Chi or other meditative and physical disciplines that can help release tension and stir creativity. Talk with other singers about your struggles. Professionals often do so, yet students rarely share their journeys. Is it because you think no one else struggles? Take a risk and find out. If you enjoy reading biographies, read about the lives of some famous singers. You may find it helpful in your own process to read how they handled the vicissitudes of singing.

Allow yourself to believe that you are so much more than any one of your abilities/talents and so much more, even, than the sum of them. Accept yourself when you fail, accept yourself when you succeed. Learn to avoid linking your self-worth to your achievements in classes, on exams, in performances, the studio or the practice room.

Perform as often as you can. It really does get easier—especially if you can look on each outing as just one more in a series of experiments. Keep a journal and write out your desires, your fears, and your goals. As you analyze the results of several performances and surrounding circumstances, you will be able to develop supportive, comforting routines for performance days, you will have a heightened sense of experimentation and a greater feeling of control over the situation.

Be gentle with yourself. When you are having one of those days when nothing goes right, do not push it if the singing does not feel good. Chances are your muscles are tight from tension. On the other hand, singing can often help us overcome our troubles. So try for a bit, but give yourself a day off if your voice does not respond.

Take an acting class. The self-discovery involved will aid you in all your singing activities and the ability to put on a character will help in all performances.

Take a risk and let go. Let the sound come out—do not push or force or make it happen. Allow it to happen. If you can let go of overthinking, of worrying, of control, if you can allow the singing to emerge, true miracles happen.

PROGRESS AND PROCESS

You may find, as you continue to study singing, that your progress feels cyclical. This is normal; you are certainly not alone. Many students begin voice study because their families, teachers, or peers have remarked on their naturally beautiful instrument. At first, it all seems *easy*. We learn new concepts quickly, we hear vast improvement in our singing, and all seems to be flowing along. Then we go through a period of feeling as if there is so much to think about, so many new sensations to be aware of, so many new coordinations to master, that we will never get better and it is all way too much, it is just hard, hard, hard. Take heart and do not give up. After some more study, it will feel easy again, only this time the ease will be based on solid technique and the ease of singing will be at a much higher level than before. Progress in such a physical, psychological, and emotional endeavor will naturally go through cycles. You may find yourself revisiting areas of technique that you had thought were mastered long ago. Again, take heart. Your progress can be viewed as similar to tightening the spokes on a bicycle wheel. When one spoke is tightened, all the others need to be adjusted as well. So once you have improved your resonance tracking, you may find that support needs to be revisited and that brings up the need for attention to posture, and so on. In most organic endeavors such as singing, the student needs to revisit concepts rather frequently. However, as you progress, your review of concepts is at a higher and higher level of expertise.

This cyclical nature of vocal progress is true of creative endeavors in general. The noted Jungian psychoanalyst, author, and lecturer, Dr. Clarissa Pinkola Estés, talks about the cycles of creativity in her recording *The Creative Fire* (see "Resources"). As is true with the seasons and many aspects of life, Estés explains that creativity goes through a cycle of birth, rising energy, a zenith, entropy, decline, death, incubation, then again birth and a new cycle.

When we feel that things are not going well, we may be in the entropy or death parts of the cycle. It is important, however, to not give up at this point. Occasionally, you might need to take a break or a vacation from singing for a short while. Yet if you are discouraged by these downswings in the cycle and use them as an excuse to avoid the work of creativity, your growth will surely be stunted. This is the discipline of being an artist—showing up, practicing, and studying on a regular basis no matter where you are in the cycle of creativity. It is this discipline that allows the muse to speak to us—that ensures that there will again be upswings in the cycle. Follow the process rather than worry about the end product.

WHY DO WE SING? REFLECTIONS ON EMOTIONS, SPIRITUALITY, AND ETHICS

Why do we sing? At first we may be pleased by the sounds we make, we might enjoy the attention and the spotlight, we may take pleasure in the physical sensations, and we might relish the sense of camaraderie when joining others in ensembles. All of these are good benefits, yet most singers who have been at it for a while will tell you that singing is ultimately much more.

Once the basic technique is in place, the whole body is involved in singing and the mind is freer to be in a meditative mode, most singers feel that their practicing, rehearsing, and performing are truly spiritual events. Those experiences can vary from time to time. Occasionally the singer might feel that the practice session has been an emotional catharsis. Other times practice or rehearsal sessions may be times of renewal and reenergizing. Most often in performance, singers report a sense of connectedness—of feeling grounded, in tune with the universe and with the people around them. Then the singing is usually described as effortless, as if the singer were the channel, the conduit for the sound. Some say they feel as if someone else were singing through them: the universe, God, spirit, or love. In the recording mentioned earlier in this chapter, Estés calls this phenomenon "luminosity": a sense of being connected with all of life and a feeling of bliss. It can be quite addictive.

Before you dismiss this as too "new age" or "woo woo," remember that singing most likely began as a spiritual activity and for many people, singing is still a part of early religious training. It evokes memories of community, of sacred moments, of times of quiet and introspection. Even for those without any connection with institutional religion, it is certainly in our genes, in our collective unconscious, to associate singing and other creative activities with spiritual matters. And, as described later in this chapter, creativity in general is an important part of our spiritual/emotional/psychological health.

I believe that music in general and singing in particular does touch something deep within us. Since singers are the instrument as well as the player, the acts of singing and of listening to it are ultimately very intimate. I would urge singers and teachers of singing to recognize this and to encourage each other to honor and respect the vulnerable, spiritual, soul-bearing act that singing can be. The spiritual aspect of singing is rarely discussed among singers. I have yet to encounter the cast of an opera or a musical sitting around backstage talking about the luminosity or catharsis they experience in the show. What they often do discuss is the end product—the performance, rather than the process. Yet I do think most seasoned singers are aware, if on an unconscious level, that their work is sacred, that when they perform they are entering holy territory. Perhaps because there is no tradition of sharing this journey and no vehicle for working through the process with others, singers sometimes are guarded or defensive or cling to strange backstage rituals. It would take some courage to start openly sharing and discussing the creative process. I wonder if the time has come for singers in college or university to begin the process of sharing their inner journeys and supporting one another.

There certainly are singers and teachers and others in the field who do not approach their art and their craft with reverence. Tales abound of undermining behavior or prima donna antics. A peek beneath the surface will reveal that these are often the acts of scared, insecure, or troubled people attempting to cover up their fear of intimacy and of being vulnerable by means of these distracting antics. Sometimes these behaviors can come from a deep well of unhappiness: if we are not happy with our own creative life, it can be hard to be happy about someone else's. And there are, after all, people with serious psychological/emotional issues that express themselves in wanting to kill creativity in themselves or in others.

What we need to remember as artists and as human beings is that, "creative life is not about success or failure. It is a mystery, a spiritual practice to live from the creative center in our everyday life."[1] In the recording mentioned earlier, Estés describes creativity and creative acts as the bridge between the center of the psyche or the inner mind and the outer world. Thus, the drive toward creativity is so important and so basic to our nature that extinguishing it in others or undermining

---

1. Estés, Clarissa Pinkola, *The Creative Fire* (Boulder, CO: Sounds True, 1991).

others' work or success need to be treated as the true violations they are and not lightly dismissed as prima donna antics or simply the behavior of a temperamental musician. People who experience huge blocks in their creativity or have these kinds of psychological problems were not born that way. The problems they experience in allowing themselves or others to create or to fully experience the creative process happen because of the negative comments, snide remarks, or other forms of rejection they experienced as children or young adults. One cutting comment may or may not produce that kind of damage. But if added to several others, it may be the negative moment that deeply injures that person. If creativity is a large part of our spiritual life, then doing anything to harm someone's creative process or endeavors is tantamount to harming their spirituality, their soul, and their very core.

The National Association of Teachers of Singing has a code of ethics that all members must endorse and follow. These standards prohibit pros-elytizing students from another studio, criticizing another teacher's work, making false promises to new students, and so on. To my mind, it boils down to: do your best work, say nothing about another teacher if you can-not say something good, be gentle and honest with your students, enjoy your work, and refrain from the grass-is-greener syndrome. It seems to me that singers could make and abide by a similar code of ethics: do your best work, say nothing about your colleagues if you cannot praise them, wait to be asked for feedback, and then critique gently and praise as much as you critique, avoid gossip, own your mistakes, and do not try to pass the blame, be prepared and on time, enjoy your work, enjoy your unique talents and abilities and refrain from the grass-is-greener syndrome. If your own creative life is unfulfilling, focus on improving it rather than being jealous of or undermining the creative life of someone else.

When we can be supportive colleagues and focus on our art without the distractions of competition and gossip then the spiritual nature of singing is heightened. We then can share our voices, our music, and ourselves in an artistic, fulfilling, and even holy act.

RESOURCES

General Information or Multiple Topics

http://www.nats.org—site of the National Association of Teachers of Singing. Information on pedagogy, conferences, workshops, finding a teacher and links to numerous singing related sites.

http://www.nfcs.net—site of the New Forum for Classical Singers. Primarily useful for information sharing and networking possibilities.

http://www.classicalsinger.com—monthly publication's site. Audition information, articles; help with finding teachers and coaches.

http://www.vocalist.org—information on repertoire, singing tips, networking, and other areas generally aimed at classical singers and teachers.

http://www.kendavies.net/musicwebhunter/index.html—site with information on many areas of music, including recordings, organizations, and related Web sites.

Body Work

http://www.alexandertechnique.com—articles, information and resources for finding a teacher.

http://www.ati-net.com—Alexander Technique International. Worldwide resources for finding a teacher as well as basic information.

http://www.feldenkraisguild.com—articles and information on the Feldenkrais Method as well as resources for finding a teacher.

http://www.feldenkrais.com—similar to site above but limited to North America.

http://www.yogajournal.com—site of *Yoga Journal* with articles, information, and resources for finding a teacher.

http://www.yimag.org—site *Yoga International Magazine* with lots of information and resources for finding a teacher.

Character Work, Translations, and Performing

Coffin, Berton, Werner Singer, and Pierre Delattre. *Word-by-Word Translations of Songs and Arias.* New York: Scarecrow Press, 1966. (Part I German and French)

Fischer-Dieskau, Dietrich. *The Fischer-Dieskau Book of Lieder.* New York: Limelight Editions, 1984.

Goldovsky, Boris. *Bringing Soprano Arias to Life.* New York: G. Schirmer, 1973.

Hagen, Uta. *Respect for Acting.* New York: Macmillan, 1973.

Helfgot, Daniel. *The Third Line.* New York: Schirmer Books, 1993.

Miller, Philip. *The Ring of Words: An Anthology of Song Texts.* New York: W.W. Norton, 1973.

Schoep, Arthur, and Daniel Harris. *Word-by-Word Translations of Songs and Arias.* New York: Scarecrow Press, 1966. (Part II: Italian)

Singher, Martial. *An Interpretive Guide to Operatic Arias.* University Park: Pennsylvania State University Press, 1983.

Creativity and the Artist's Life

Cameron, Julia. *The Artist's Way.* New York: Tarcher/Putnam, 2002.

Estés, Clarissa Pinkola. *The Creative Fire.* Boulder, CO: Sounds True, 1991. Audio tape.

Rilke, Rainer Maria. *Letters to a Young Poet.* New York: W.W. Norton, 2004.

Sher, Barbara and Annie Gottlieb. *Wishcraft: How to Get What You Really Want.* New York: Ballantine, 1986.

Fächer

http://en.wikipedia.org/wiki/Fach

Sullivan, Gail, and Dorothy Maddison. *Kein' Angst Baby!* New York: Clearing Press, 1994.

Learning Modalities

http://library.thinkquest.org/C005704/content_hwl_learningmodalities.php3

http://712educators.about.com/cs/learnstyleassess/index.htm

Balk, H. Wesley. *Performing Power.* Mineapolis: University of Minnesota Press, 1985, 66.

Music Reading Fundamentals

http://datadragon.com/education/reading

Musical Scores:
Suggested Volumes

Boytim, Joan Frey (ed). *The First Book of Solos* (four volumes: soprano, mezzo, tenor, bass). New York: G. Schirmer, 1994. (More volumes for each voice type *The First Book of Solos Part II, The Second Book of Solos.*)

Musical Theatre Classics. (Two volumes for each voice type). Milwaukee, WI: Hal Leonard, 1996.

Niles, John Jacob. *The Songs of John Jacob Niles* (two volumes: high voice and low voice). New York: G. Schirmer, 1993.

Paton, John Glen (ed). *Twenty-six Italian Songs and Arias* (two volumes: medium-high and medium-low). Van Nuys, CA: Alfred Publishing, 1991.

Walters, Richard (ed.). *The Singer's Musical Theatre Anthology* (2 volumes for each voice type of soprano, mezzo, tenor, bass plus one book of duets). Milwaukee, WI: Hal Leonard, 1993.

Online Ordering Possibilities

http://www.brodtmusiconline.com or 800-438-4129— knowledgeable staff, good service.
http://www.classicalvocalrep.com or 800-298-7474— excellent service. Glendower Jones is highly knowledgeable and handles only vocal music. Good for all repertoire as well as obscure pieces and out-of-print works.
http://www.ebay.com— good for opera scores especially and if you are looking for something unusual or out-of-print.
http://www.tismusic.com—a large selection of vocal scores.

Musicians' and Actors' Unions

American Guild of Musical Artists (AGMA): http://www.musicalartists.org
American Federation of Television and Radio Artists (AFTRA): http://www.aftra.org
Actors Equity Association (AEA): http://www.actorsequity.org

Professionalism and the Business of Singing

Dornemann, Joan. *Complete Preparation.* New York: Excalibur, 1992.
Kirkpatrick, Carol. *Aria Ready.* Mt. Morris, NY: Leyerle, 2003.
Papolos, Janice. *The Performing Artist's Handbook.* Cincinnati, OH: Writer's Digest, 1984.
Sullivan, Gail, and Dorothy Maddison. *Kein' Angst Baby!* New York: Clearing Press, 1994.

Technique/Pedagogy

Alderson, Richard. *The Complete Handbook of Voice Training.* West Nyack, NY: Parker, 1979.
Brown, Oren. *Discover Your Voice.* San Diego: Singular Publishing Group, 1996.
Cheng, Stephen Chun-Tao. *The Tao of Voice.* Rochester, VT: Destiny Books, 1991.
Kagen, Sergius. *On Studying Singing.* New York: Dover Press, 1950.
Miller, Richard. *The Structure of Singing.* Belmont, CA: Wadsworth Group, 1996. (Many more books by this author, including volumes devoted to specific voice types.)

Vocal Health

Brodnitz, Friedrich. *Keep Your Voice Healthy.* Boston: Little, Brown, 1988.
Davies, D. Garfield, and Anthony F. Jahn. *Care of the Professional Voice.* Oxford: Butterworth/ Heinemann, 1998.
The National Center for Voice and Speech: http://www.ncvs.org/
The Center for Voice Disorders: http://www1.wfubmc.edu/voice

Voice Teachers

http://www.nats.org
http://classicalsinger.com
http://www.privatelessons.com
http://www.voiceteachers.com

PERFORMANCE ANXIETY
An Annotated Bibliography

Bruser, Madeline. *Art of Practicing, The*. New York: Bell Tower, 1997. Subtitled: *A Guide to Making Music from the Heart*. Making music with your whole self, enjoying practicing, savoring music moment by moment: these and other concepts are presented to rekindle our love for music. Not waiting until just before a performance to think of expression and emotion, but bringing our whole selves to our practicing makes the journey more enjoyable and reduces performance anxiety, too. Well worth reading.

Gallwey, W. Timothy. *Inner Game of Tennis, The*. New York: Random House, 1974. A gem! There's a reason this book has been in print for over thirty years. You need not be an athlete (I have never played tennis in my life) to profit from Gallwey's suggestions. It is easy to draw mental parallels with performing and the book is an enjoyable read, to boot.

Green, Barry. *Inner Game of Music, The*. Anchor Press, 1986. Based on Gallweys' book in this list, but without its clean style and readability. Some good ideas specific to music, however, and worth at least a quick read-through.

Greene, Don. *Audition Success*. New York: ProMind Music, 1998. Subtitled: *An Olympic Sports Psychologist Teaches Performing Artists How to Win*. I found this to be highly readable and informative. The book chronicles the story of two musicians (a French horn player and a Mezzo) as they prepare for auditions and performances. The transcribed conversations are full of ideas to apply to your own practicing and preparation without the overpedantic style of many books on this subject.

Greene, Don. *Fight Your Fear and Win–A 21-Day Plan*. New York: Broadway Books, 2001. Subtitled: *7 Skills for Performing Your Best Under Pressure-at Work, in Sports, on Stage*. I would read either *Inner Game of Tennis* or *Soprano on Her Head* to start the process/journey of working on performance anxiety. I think this book is for someone who has already worked on some performance issues and is ready for a real "battle plan". Includes a seven skills profile (determination, energy, perspective, courage, focus, poise, resilience) and a Web site for scoring the quiz. Then we are equipped to focus on only those areas that need improvement, with plenty of ideas and approaches for improvement.

Greene, Don. *Performance Success*. New York: Routledge, 2002. As with *Fight Your Fear* (above), this book includes a skills profile and a Web site for scoring the quiz. It, too, is a 21-day plan but this time focused on preparing for a performance and overcoming anxiety along the way. The reader is asked to find a mentor and to participate in a rigorous and structured plan. This may be a great approach to take before a high-stakes event: a debut performance or a degree-culminating recital.

Krüger, Irmtraud Tarr. *Performance Power.* Tempe, AZ: Summit Books, 1993. Currently out of print, but worth looking for. Dr. Krüger is both a psychotherapist and a performer (organ) with plenty of information to give on the manifestations of performance anxiety physiologically and psychologically. She also offers good preparation techniques, relaxation exercises and even some "quick-fixes".

Lieberman, Julie Lyonn. *You Are Your Instrument.* New York: Huiksi Music, 1991. Written for instrumentalists as well as singers, this book offers fresh ideas. Especially useful are suggestions for using the whole person in practice and integrating both right and left-brain hemispheres in performance. Very different from the other books on this list and worth a read-through.

Ristad, Eloise. *Soprano on Her Head, A.* Moab, UT: Real People Press, 1982. The BIBLE, really. Don't be deceived by the title, it's for instrumentalists, actors, dancers, all performers. Great ideas for practicing, preparation and performing. I have often given copies of this book to nonperformers, because, as the subtitle says, it's *Right-Side-Up Reflections on Life and Other Performances.*

ABOUT THE AUTHOR

Sharon L. Stohrer is on the voice faculty of the Department of Music and Performing Arts Professions, Steinhardt School of Education at New York University. She also teaches voice privately and presents workshops on overcoming performance anxiety. For more information, please visit her Web site: http://www.sharonstohrer.com.

INDEX